A Story of Addiction, Awareness and Ascension

Deborah G. Edwards

Cover Design by JetLaunch.net

Edited by Elizabeth Lyons

High / Deborah G. Edwards — 1st ed.

ISBN 978-1-7344943-5-7 (pbk)
ISBN 978-1-7344043-4-0 (eBook)

Disclaimer

The content of this book is not intended to be a substitute for professional medical advice, diagnosis, or treatment. Always seek the advice of a physician or other qualified health provider with any questions you may have regarding a medical condition or addiction.

Neither the author nor the publisher shall be liable for misuse of this material. This book is strictly for informational and educational purposes.

Dedicated to my son, Andrew Conner Jurek. Our souls, our journeys were meant to be intertwined. Your heart, resilience, and courage continue to inspire me. I love you a zillion times around the universe!

A constant state of prayer. That's how I live. Prayer, in my view, is consistent communion and conversation with God. There isn't a process, an order, or a set of rules for me regarding prayer.

For me, it's quieting my mind enough to feel into my body, then my soul. It's slowing myself enough to connect fully to my being in separation from the world around me and all that may be going on in my life. It's then opening myself in stillness to hear.

I've pleaded and expressed frustrations. I've brought in the sense of connectedness and peace. I've patiently and impatiently waited for wisdom, for what feels like truth from all that is divine.

This, for me, is a constant state of prayer, and it is the most important piece of my human existence puzzle.

CONTENTS

Foreword..1
Introduction..5
CHAPTER 1 17
CHAPTER 2 27
CHAPTER 3 31
CHAPTER 4 39
CHAPTER 5 47
CHAPTER 6 53
CHAPTER 7 61
CHAPTER 8 69
CHAPTER 9 85
CHAPTER 10 89
CHAPTER 11 95
CHAPTER 12 101
CHAPTER 13 113
CHAPTER 14 127
CHAPTER 15 129
CHAPTER 16 141
CHAPTER 17 145
CHAPTER 18 169
CHAPTER 19 181
CHAPTER 20 187

CHAPTER 21 193
CHAPTER 22 197
CHAPTER 23 207
CHAPTER 24 215
CHAPTER 25 231
CHAPTER 26 237
CHAPTER 27 247
CHAPTER 28 255
CHAPTER 29 267
About the Author 275
Acknowledgements 277

FOREWORD

On a warm spring day in 2018, I had my first meeting with Deborah Edwards (at Starbucks, naturally). We'd connected a few weeks prior—during the four minutes we both coincidentally spent engaging in a Facebook group that neither of us visited with any frequency whatsoever—and it just so happened that she was in town on business. Having arrived a few minutes early, I ordered an iced green tea and noticed that the barista's name was Libby. My childhood nickname was Libby, and until that point, I'd only ever met two other women with the same moniker. The moment I told Libby No. 3 this, she wrote "Libby" on my cup, and it should have become immediately apparent that I was about to embark on one heck of an adventure.

Several times I've heard it theorized that before we come into this life, we have a plan—one based on a clear understanding of what we are coming here to learn. To teach. To experience. At the moment our life as human beings starts, however, we forget about that plan, and the journey thereafter is all about remembering. While perhaps aggravating, the instantaneous forgetting is also by design, also a component of the experience to which we agreed.

As far as I'm concerned, Deborah Edwards never fully forgot, even in the moments when she didn't recognize that she had remembered. She is a remarkably unique woman. And yet, she's incredibly similar in many ways to you and to me. She's down-to-earth, steady, intentional. She's also unsure and hesitant while managing an inner turbulence as strong as it is invisible to others. And that's one of the greatest lessons: What is going on inside is only truly known by the one experiencing it.

At her core, Deborah Edwards is persistently aware, intentional, and courageously curious. And that is where the magic of this story lies. I don't know if I could handle such a series of unimaginable events with the grace, determination, and stoicism Deborah employed. When I consider the mental and emotional strength required to let go with love and simply allow and consider what a gamble that was for her, I (as a parent myself) have such a deep reverence for the gifts available to all of us in her approach to life. It sometimes makes me wonder if part of my own plan was to come into contact with her at this precise time in my own journey so that I could take some of her methods with me into my own day-to-day challenges, both comfortable and not-so-much.

A point I hope to make abundantly clear—because our initial instinct is often to regard addicts with distrust and quickly adopt a "that will never happen to my kid" attitude: Andrew Jurek is an extraordinary young man. He's also not terribly different from the accomplished boy next door, the magnificent son you're raising, or the incredible kid who taught your kid to swim or kick a soccer ball or determine the square root of pi. I've had multiple conversations with him during which I was certain I was speaking to a wise old man in a twenty-seven-year-old's body. He's living his life in this way, at least in great part, because his mother allowed it. I mean that in the most literal of ways: She took what has to be the most difficult approach by *allowing* the journey to unfold, by allowing his soul to travel in the way it intended to travel.

Few stories have opened my eyes the way this one has. It's repeatedly provided the kind of "crack in the egg" moments I live for—the moments when you are blessed with a newly colored perspective toward something you've seen in shades of gray all your life. I am grateful for my newfound outlooks on addiction, on forgiveness, on presence, and on patience—truly transformed perspectives that can never be undone.

May you take from this story every word that resonates with you as well as each technique that you didn't know you absolutely needed to employ in your life. May you have a newfound reverence for the challenges your fellow humans face, especially the ones you judge while truly knowing nothing about them. May you recognize that the reason you often judge them isn't that you truly disapprove as much as it is that you're afraid of them happening to you, and that belief is simply too painful to rationally or logically sift through the sieve. May you be reminded that in every challenge there is an opportunity. May you hold dear that, in the end, as Ram Dass so beautifully stated, we're all just walking each other home.

Elizabeth Lyons, Author of *Enough: The Simple Path to Everything You Want*
Phoenix, Arizona
April 5, 2020

INTRODUCTION

I wonder sometimes if, in that moment, the moment I saw that look in his eyes, I knew where we were headed. That a life-altering darkness was approaching, a season that would rock us to our core. I wonder, What could I have done differently? Because that was the moment. That was when I saw it, even though I didn't really know what it was.

My father was a lifelong alcoholic, and the last few years of his life were downhill all the way. I was his one and only person; there was simply no one else there for him in those years. During the holiday season of 2010, both my uncle and my dad were in the hospital—my uncle in San Diego, my dad in Arizona. My uncle had suffered a seizure, and my dad had been in the hospital for a while due to complications from a pacemaker that, let's be honest, were the ultimate result of decades of consistent drinking with reckless abandon. I felt completely torn about where to be until I heard something in my auntie's voice that told me she needed me, a pain that was hard to ignore. After my dad assured me that he was okay (my auntie was his sister, after all), I drove from the hospital in Arizona to San Diego to see my uncle.

We got a few things taken care of, among them realizing he would need a wheelchair from that point forward and made arrangements to have a ramp installed at his house. Two days later I drove back to Arizona and went straight to the hospital to see my dad. Unbelievably, the doctor was standing right outside my dad's room when I walked in, and he said he needed to talk to me.

My dad had nine lives. He shouldn't have lived nearly as long as he did, given the way he abused his body. I knew he was struggling, and I knew that he was in worse health than he'd ever been, but I'd seen him come back from the brink so many times that I was confident I would return to discover that he was on the upswing. The chances of my arrival from California perfectly coinciding with the doctor's presence outside my dad's room was nothing short of divine, and it solidified my faith in divine presence.

My father was dying. We moved him to hospice, and after five days, he passed.

Fast-forward a year, and the normally festive 2011 holiday season rounded out what had already been a challenging year—and that's putting it mildly. Just two months after my father died, my uncle, who had been the much better father-figure in my life, followed suit. In between those two losses, my son, Andrew—my only child—had been arrested three times for possession of marijuana, allowing me to experience our criminal court system with a level of frequency that interests no one. He was now addicted to heroin. My husband and I had filed for bankruptcy, lost our home, and were headed for divorce.

Andrew's story is such a magnificent piece of the tapestry of my own life. It was, by far, the hardest circumstance I've yet encountered. It's through our challenges, however, that we get to figure out what we're truly made of. No matter what, I always want to do that well. For sure, whatever my "well" is in each moment will differ, but my intention is to handle any challenge that crosses my path to the best of my ability.

While one might wonder why I'd write about all of this—let alone why they'd want to read about it all—I'd propose that I've become particularly skilled at navigating some pretty clunky things in life. Most of what I've learned came without a guide, and I've developed some strategies that I believe can benefit others, including the practice of presence; observant listening; patient love; prayerful availability, living experientially; and vigorously pursuing your self, your path, and your truth.

There tends to be a badge of shame—self-imposed or otherwise—worn by people who have family members battling addiction. There are also many stories that, heartbreakingly, don't turn out well. More people don't make it out than do. Too many people, good people, lose their lives. Some people aren't able to get themselves beyond the dysfunction, and they aren't interested in working a program or seeing professional help to help them navigate it. My own father was one of those people. I've learned so much from living through the brutality of it all, and I want to share my journey with the hope that people will glean a tip that helps them better navigate their journey as well as accept permission to be happy—even after chaos has cemented itself as part of their adventure on this planet.

When I think about the hundreds of thousands of people in the world who are battling—or have loved ones battling—some form of harmful addiction, be it alcoholism, drug addiction, or one of the less substance-related but equally damaging diseases like anorexia or bulimia, I feel an enormous world-body woundedness. This is what it is—a woundedness—and we have given it a shame-based false meaning that no longer serves us. The health of our mind is just as important as, if not more important than, the health of our body.

When you have a loved one battling addiction, especially when that person is your child, and you're in the depths of this incredible experience, you have feelings of hopelessness, of desperation, of not knowing how to contend with or make sense with the enormousness of what the fear and pain feels like. You just want it to stop, and it seems like it's not going to. Now that we are where we are, I'm grateful to be able to ask Andrew what he was going through in certain moments. It's important to me that he be able to express his perspective, and because I believe that having regard for the other side of an experience might also help others, and I've included Andrew's thoughts as appropriate throughout the book.

To be clear, the ugly pieces of one's challenges don't have to involve addiction. We live in a world full of judgement, and therefore, shoulds and shame manifest every day in the threads that sew our souls together after loss, tragedy, and generally poor choices. While those feelings can easily compel us to go further inward, shrinking into a place we might believe is safer, that approach in no way serves us. It's up to us to find the vine of power within the losses, the tragedies, and the crazy moments in which we find ourselves. That vine is there every single time. And once discovered and claimed, it becomes unbreakable.

The more we can each embrace the uglier pieces of the road we walk, the more ease there will be in our lives. We tend to fight against difficult experiences, but those experiences infiltrate our lives by design; they are here for our gain, our evolution, to resurrect the gemstones that live inside each of us.

Regardless of what's happening around you, you have within you everything you need to prevail. You're more capable than your current belief system tells you that you are of handling events even harder than those you're currently experiencing. Pivotal moments occur when you're watching loved ones dying or falling toward addiction or being less than completely honest with you, and those are the moments you have to approach in love and with strength while still holding space for the belief that a better outcome is possible. The journey as well as the outcome might end up looking a little different than you expected, but it's possible for it to be glorious, nonetheless. The approach will challenge you to your core, but, if we're being honest, so will many other things.

The nucleus of my life philosophy is, fiercely pursue your truth, your path, your flight. This pursuit requires an uncovering of what matters most to you, your deepest desires and dreams. It requires an uncovering of your strengths, talents, values, preferences, "Oh hell yes" moments, and "Oh hell no" moments. It requires clarity around your interests, your inspirations, your passions, and your boundaries, and an understanding of both what's true for you and what isn't. It requires an uncovering of the shine and the spark in your soul.

There are likely people who see this kind of self-priority as selfish, even negative. I remember, when I was younger, overhearing several men in my dad's circle having a conversation and being sarcastic about the notion that "she left because she had to find herself." In truth, their cynicism isn't far off; we are all here to do just that: discover ourselves and others in and through the energy of love. And from that place, unearth and share our contribution with the world. Life itself is the ultimate soul refinery.

However, if we could all show up from this place of fullness—standing fully in the shine of our soul, where we are so connected to those things that are truly us, not merely what society tells us we should or should not be or do—we would each be able to give so very much more.

To be clear, I am in no way suggesting that we all become self-focused individuals at the expense of being there for others. That, in fact, is when we feel love the most—when we are engaged in the act of loving. What I'm suggesting is that, when we are so disconnected from our true center, when we are so fragmented because we have spent more time focused on others and not enough time coming to intimately know and love ourselves, we cannot love at our full capacity.

We can go through periods in life when we feel completely lost. But, through faith that the path will ultimately unfold for our best possible outcomes, we trudge through. This faithful thinking gives us fuel for the swamp-walking, the darker times. When people find themselves at the precipice, when they're at their absolute worst point, some fall toward making things better and some fall toward making them far worse. I fell toward the former—not because I'm inherently strong but because I was determined. That determination revealed many opportunities to grab courage and take action while holding belief. From that approach, my strength grew.

What's more, we—each and every one of us—are writing our own stories, literally and figuratively, every single day. The full body of my soul feels bathed in gratitude for it all, including the darkest times, because it brought me here.

Don't get me wrong; sadness and hard emotions are part of the deal. But I have seen too many people resign in the face of sadness, my father being the best example of that in my own life. Some resign themselves to a set of very different choices; to a set of conclusions that create or reinforce beliefs that do not serve them; to the letting go of the pursuit of things that make them feel alive, happy, and joyful. In my world, that kind of resignation is flat-out messed up. There is a gift in every experience, and that gift is seen in both the vine of power and the gorgeous growth that are there for the taking. Ultimately, it's the gift of our evolution as individuals. And a collective evolution, side by side by side, is what has the power to move humanity forward. I made one simple decision in the midst of the insanity churning around me: I drew a more empowering conclusion, which was, in the most simplistic version, "The path to happiness is mine to walk."

I wanted to and was determined to realize the

higher vision for my life, and I declared that I'd unpack the lesson from every one of the experiences to come. I vowed to boldly warrior my way through the resulting swamp water from that incredibly difficult year until I reached the desert, and then the runway. And then, I took off from there, and experienced the joy that comes from finally taking flight. Again and again and again.

People often ask how I managed everything. After all, so many messed-up life experiences in such a short window creates some pretty brutal living. What I now understand is that each small piece of the puzzle was its own contribution to the masterpiece of my life, of our life. I'm no different from anybody else who has experiences that show up unexpectedly. We each have our regular, everyday life, and then we have this "stuff" (I like to refer to them as "situations") that comes and sits down right next to that regular life (and sometimes, on top of it). It's about what you do on a daily—sometimes hourly—basis to get through it all. Sometimes you laugh at the end of the day because it's all you can do. And sometimes tears come.

Regardless of what you're going through in life, there are ways you can navigate it powerfully. And the space from which you navigate it powerfully is a much better-feeling and empowered place to be than the alternative. You get to choose whether or not to navigate it from that place. You can be empowered or disempowered. The switch is always yours to flip.

Maybe your challenge isn't having a son on heroin. Maybe it's lighter, or maybe it's "worse." When someone is going through the hardest thing they've ever gone through, it's the hardest thing they've ever gone through for precisely that reason. It's an in-the-mirror comparison, not a comparison with everyone else with whom they come into contact. At that point in time, it's the hardest thing they've ever gone through—even if the issue is as "small" as having incredibly dirty windows. There are people who haven't had many difficult experiences by others' determination, and it can be easy to think, "Come on, how hard is that really?" But we have to remember that because they've had relatively few experiences, this is that difficult for them. And we don't get to judge that.

Before now, before this place where my son and I have both overcome so much, I was in no way ready to tell this story. It's a level of vulnerability I've never before stepped into. Whether or not my words resonate with you, whether or not judgement makes its way in, whether or not there is criticism, I can no longer hold it in. Because someone is sitting in their own dark room, and they need to know that the light switch is just a reach away. Over time and with intention, the darkness in my life turned into the light in my life. The seasons we go through can feel like a darkening, an abrupt sunset. If you allow yourself to move through it from a different place, beginning from a clean slate, the light moves back in and becomes brighter, one moment at a time.

If you're in the midst of a challenge that seems unnavigable, I want you to know that your story can have a different outcome. By all logic, Andrew should be in jail. Or, far worse, dead. I could be homeless or still scraping by. There could have been a million different outcomes, for both him and me, and you don't have to—in your frustration and pain—resign yourself to an outcome you don't want. The specific details of your challenges are unique to you. But it is my hope that some of my principles, my truths, and my guiding lights will help you navigate your journey as you commit to your own fierce pursuit of flight.

CHAPTER 1

When bad things happen, some people will say it's one's karma from this life, or perhaps another life. I believe that some situations just arrive. I believe there absolutely is a divine interaction as we move through our human life. I also believe in the result of the energy that comes from both love and fear. I believe that the thoughts that create that energy have an outcome. But I don't believe in penalty, or that life is punitive. I don't believe it all boils down to "right living" or "wrong living." I believe we carry our experiences with us, and we can make those experiences heavy, burdensome, and painful, or we can turn them inside out and use them for our gain and the gain of others. When viewed in that way, they're all blessings.

If you were to continue to walk through your whole life in the pain body of all of your harder experiences, you'd be choosing for them to travel through life with you in a way that robs you of the moments that bring you joy. After all, that's the energy that you've both created and surrounded yourself with in some way by choosing this. We each want to speculate about how this whole "life" thing works, and when all is said and done, it works however it does. The human experience is an ever-evolving one. Your being continues to expand and contract its energy, love, and fear, and we can each impact that expansion and contraction differently. If we all could grasp this concept and stop with the "rightness" and "wrongness" of it all, the world would be an entirely different place.

These days, much focus is put on the importance of being present in the now. But there's another layer we must place on top of the now, and it's a critical one. The emphasis on being present in the now is valid, but there's also a more energy-centric, deeper level of being in the now that requires a greater attunement to oneself and what's actually occurring. Being *truly* present is an experiential act. It's not accomplished simply by being knowledgeable about "being present"; it's about *truly, fully experiencing the moment that you are in.*

We most need the ability to tune in to this kind of presence *before* we realize we've landed square in the thick of it. In those instances, we don't have time to sit in meditation and get calm. We have to be able to experience presence in the midst of the chaos, and that is a skill that is honed.

We are amazing beings with an internal app that needs a serious update. We're running on an outdated system, one we most certainly wouldn't intentionally purchase today. So, you could look at self-work as a method of creating system fixes within ourselves, and doing that with love is to not lose patience with yourself or the process of it.

Oftentimes in growth, first comes healing, and that's not something you can warrior through, my friend. It's not something you can control. Healing is something you make space for. It's something you give freedom to so it can come, when and how it needs to. It's not always pretty. In fact, it oftentimes has some very ugly moments that attach as permanently as war wounds, but it's also glorious, bestowing its beauty at the same time. That's how I think of it when I look back: The journey to now, to this moment, was glorious. Fierce love doesn't apply only to the way we love others; it also applies to the way we love ourselves, and when you are in a healing phase, it is an absolute necessity.

We all arrived here on this earth equipped to endure our battles and emerge stronger. There is a source greater than ourselves available to us in every moment of every hour. We too easily forget that as well as the importance of relying on not just our own strength but also the strength of those around us. You'll find whatever you need within this beautifully woven humanity through an almost silent reliance on something greater than our humanness.

It's a matter of allowing yourself to breathe and be open to what is available. It's allowing yourself to love yourself enough in the horrible moment you're experiencing to be able to take the next step. And, more importantly, to both own and fiercely protect your state of belief, no matter what. Sometimes, that act in and of itself—allowing yourself to simply and fully love yourself while protecting your belief—requires the most strength.

In order to best show where my philosophies were both birthed and honed over the years, it's best that I share a bit about my childhood and adolescence. The foundation they laid was tantamount to the way I would ultimately navigate not only Andrew's addiction but the many other tsunami-like moments that have befallen my life.

I grew up with one sister named Julie. She was twenty-two months older than I and my main point of connection as a young girl. Julie was somewhat adventurous and very curious. I was more conservative, more observational, and both fascinated by and somewhat fearful of people. We had a close relationship, but we were very different from one another. I was hopelessly driven by my feelings, always worrying about what other people were going to think. I didn't try many things because Julie was so good at anything and everything, and in hindsight, I definitely held myself back. Julie, on the other hand, did not, and yet she was so sensitive and disconnected from most people. Having said that, she was willing to explore herself and what was available to her through art and writing and music and dance. Even through all the years feeling afraid I'd never measure up to her, she always made me feel accepted.

Sometimes, I wonder how things might have been different if someone of significance had said to me, "Just be brave. Don't just put your toe in the water. Jump. Just try." I was so plagued by fear that I didn't try very much of anything. My room was (almost) always super clean, and my school locker completely organized, both because that's what was required by my father and because it reflected my never-ending attempt to be good enough.

When it came to people, I was the outgoing one. But, when it came to matters of the inner being; exploring self and one's interests, creativity, and intellect, that was Julie's area to shine. She was more socially introverted, but from a true talent perspective, from the perspective of honoring what's uniquely inside each of us, she explored her soul in ways that I didn't.

She and my mom had a kind of relationship that my mom and I didn't have, and I had a relationship with my dad that he and Julie didn't have. I would watch my mom and Julie reading together on the couch, and back then I thought they were weird to be sitting on the couch reading. But there was a piece of me that craved whatever it was they were experiencing. Having said that, what I absolutely loved was working on projects with my father. Cement slabs, room additions, landscape design—I just loved watching, learning, and being given a job to do in the pursuit of these projects. He was good at it, and he was also good at enrolling people to help. I have many fond memories with the exception of one: river rock shoveling; I didn't like that at all.

I remember when my sixth-grade teacher, Mrs. Propstra, called me up to her desk one day. She was frustrated with me because I was a little bit too—shall we say—talkative. She told me that I didn't apply myself, and at the time I didn't even understand what that meant. I just stood there thinking, "I'm going to get in trouble. I don't know what she's saying to me, but whatever it is I hope Dad doesn't get mad." When I think back to that day, I recognize that not applying myself was a spot-on description for a big chunk of that first part of my life. I was frozen by fear. No one ever told me outright that I wasn't good enough; they told me that simply by acknowledging all of my imperfections. Their intention wasn't to make me question whether or not I *was* good enough, it was to help me become better. However, focusing on a person's flaws or failings does not, nor will it ever, have the same results as focusing on their talents, their strengths. This I know to be true, and it is a big reason why I do what I do today, professionally speaking.

My dad was an interesting combination of wisdom, love, anger, and fear. He had high expectations; he was fierce. But he was also gregarious and funny and loving and wise, which was quite confusing. I always knew I was loved, and yet I always felt not good enough. He was a bit of a harsh physical disciplinarian, and his punishment tool of choice was his leather belt, complete with holes and a metal buckle.

There was only one occasion I remember when my dad actually hit me instead of whipping my ass. I had disrespected my mom, and when he got home, he clocked me upside the head so hard that I lost my balance and almost fell to the ground. It hurt something terrible, but the internal feelings that began to spin out of control were worse than the physical pain. I was frozen, slightly twisted to the right with my head down, hair hanging over my face, paralyzed with fear that if I moved, I would be hit again. So I didn't move a muscle. To this day, thinking about that moment makes my heart ache. It was a moment that sliced into my soul.

The fierceness of his parenting methods was his way (I think) of trying to build in us respect, determination, resilience, and excellence, perhaps. And, in a way, it worked more for me than for Julie, but it came at a very high price: a large amount of self-doubt, fear, and significant trust issues with essentially all human beings. My dad's nature and general way of parenting came, I believe, in part from both his alcoholism and in part from his upbringing. There was more than one experience (of which I know, anyway) when my dad got the crap beaten out of him by his own father. Ironically, the Gerards were voted Family of the Year by the Orange County something-or-other, and in the photo taken in honor of that award, they truly resembled the perfect family.

My dad was all about how things looked, just as his mom had been. I'm convinced that his obsession with the perception of himself and our family was part of what had him so screwed up. His world revolved around others' perceptions. Even if he earned good money and was a wise and loving person, his final judgements about himself were all based on his perceptions of others' perceptions, most of which were skewed to the negative. In addition, the way he mentally framed everything and then passed it through his self-loathing filter was something I simply didn't understand. My mom was much softer than my dad. She simply deferred and fell in lockstep with him because he was such a dominator. Much of what she did was with the intention not to invoke his anger. In fairness, there were many beautiful things about both of my parents. I will also add that my own mother's resilience over the years has been a truly impactful example for me. This woman has had five strokes, is in a wheelchair, has all her mental faculties, and finds a way to make almost every day a good day. That takes deep strength.

The perceptions, opinions, and judgments of others can be a surprisingly negative motivator, and they can cause us to draw inaccurate conclusions and make choices that are not only not true for us but can also often be harmful to our inner being. It's vital that we become mindful in these moments, because the perceptions and opinions most important to your life are your own. What *you* think about you is what matters most, period. Let me state it another way: What I think about me is more important to me than what *you* think about me. And let me be very clear—I don't mean this in a sense of conceit. I mean this in a sense of genuinely loving and having a pure, clear, and precise observation of who you are, where you are, and where you're headed. I discovered much later in life how vital that observation is to my happiness—to my very existence, in fact.

When we were younger, after Julie and I did our chores we'd walk around the house and joke about looking for imperfections, like a single streak on the smoky glass table. We'd laugh, but never wanted our dad to hear us because, if he did, our asses would have ended up a brilliant shade of purple. Nothing was ever quite good enough for him. When we were told to pick the weeds from the backyard, Dad wouldn't let us water the soil to make it easier to pull them. We lived in Arizona, where the ground is hard as prehistoric rock. Julie would whine and complain and end up being sent to her room, where she wanted to be anyway. She would read or play with her model horses, a pastime that would have bored me to tears.

I, on the other hand, was so stubborn—I'm a Leo through and through—and no one heard any of that whining and complaining from me. Not often anyway. I would sit out there for hours, digging deep enough with both the tool and my soil-stained fingers to excise each weed at its roots. I wanted the yard to be completely clear so that my dad would come out and say, "Wow! That's a great job!" It was as though I was waiting to hear those words from God himself, and nothing felt better than receiving them.

CHAPTER 2

November 24, 1980 brought a pain I could never have imagined. It was my first real earthquake-like life experience, a day so vividly etched in my soul that just thinking about it brings back the reel as if I am watching the movie on the biggest screen in existence.

It wasn't my parents' divorce, which happened when I was a sophomore in high school. It wasn't the challenge that came with attending three different high schools while moving between one parent's home and another's. It wasn't even my father's alcoholism and its resulting behaviors. These things all impacted my life significantly, but they in no way compared to what I experienced and what resulted from the events of that day.

It was a sunny day, and I was in a particularly high-spirited mood. Things were starting to click for me in my new high school (the third one, for the record), and I had started to feel connected to a few friend circles that brought me a feeling of belonging. There was something special about this school, and while I didn't know it then, many members of this amazing class of people, the Washington Rams of

1981, would become a life-long part of my tribe.

On that day, I had taken the bus to work after school. I worked at a clothing store called Pic-a-dilly (the name still cracks me up) at Christown Mall. When I arrived, my boss said that my mom had called and I needed to call her back. I didn't really notice it at the time, but looking back, she had a look of concern on her face that I didn't pick up on. I figured that my mom just wanted to know what time I was getting off that night because she would be the one to pick me up after work, given that I was living with her at the time.

Oddly, I didn't pay attention to the ominous sound in my boss Bethany's voice when she asked me again, "Did you call your mom?" I was walking toward the front of the store, planning to go to Peter Piper Pizza a few doors down for my favorite salad—the one with a delicious, creamy, just-the-right-amount-drizzled-on blue cheese dressing—when I saw her. My dad had remarried, and the way that my stepmom was approaching the store told me everything I needed to know. I instinctively began to back up while she continued approaching, knowing that I didn't want to hear whatever it was that she had to say. I looked behind me, and my bosses as well as the district manager were approaching me, tears falling from their eyes, my bags held in their hands. I wondered, *Why are they carrying my things?*

I turned back toward my stepmom to hear the

words that would pierce my soul and change me forever.

"Get your stuff. Get your stuff, Deb, your sister is dead." That's how I learned that my person, the one and only person I ever truly trusted, was gone from my life. Forever.

CHAPTER 3

Julie was nineteen when she died. She lived in an old apartment building with a gas-powered space heater. The windows were nailed shut, and for whatever reason, the ventilation was blocked off. She and her boyfriend both died from asphyxiation. At least I knew that they just fell asleep and didn't know what was happening to them. I have a friend whose brother and girlfriend were horrifically murdered as well as another friend whose brother suffered the same circumstance. I think that an ordeal such as that would spawn an even deeper crevasse of anger-laced pain. So, in a way, the way they died was a gift, odd as that may sound.

The loss of my sister marked the beginning of my strength-honing journey the way X marks the spot on a treasure map. While she did seemingly everything right and with ease, my undeniable specialty was people. I think I had early-onset compassion and appreciation for others, having played such an observant role for most of my life. The problem was, I'd always been too damn afraid. I went through a lot of tortured moments, thinking that other people had unique talents that God simply didn't give me. It was some seriously messed-up thinking, and what I didn't realize at the time was that those who seemed to have been blessed with more talent than I was actually just practiced that "thing" more than I did and were willing to—even if only in their own mind—fail. Nevertheless, my "people talents" allowed me to see others in the purest sense, a trait that would come to have inestimable purpose.

Julie passed right before Thanksgiving of my senior year in high school. That New Year's Eve I had my first drink, and the next day I had my first hangover. What I learned from that experience was that I could numb away my pain. I had also been introduced to marijuana, which was even better because it had no calories. My weight had been a constant creator of insecurity, so this low-calorie numbness appealed to me. That's how I dealt with her death at first: I numbed myself. Otherwise, all I felt was this deep abyss of pain, as if somebody had reached a thorn-covered hand into my body and physically ripped my soul right out.

In the aftermath of Julie's death, I didn't graduate from high school. I went to summer school in an attempt to catch up and graduate, but I wasn't in any better shape after a month of that routine. I was still trying to make sense of what had happened when earthquake number two transpired.

Less than a year after Julie passed away, I was sexually assaulted by two boys I met through a friend.

Understandably I'm sure, a lot of damage resulted from those two experiences occurring so closely together. Yet I found myself surprisingly maintaining a certain balance between being in a complete state of questioning shock and a space of deep introspection, asking, "What do I *do* with these experiences? What could possibly be here for me in all of this? Why would this happen to me? Is life at all safe? Are men safe? What do I need to pay attention to?" That's when the practice of conscious self-examination became a constant in my life, as did a thick wall of non-trusting, protective energy.

I was blessed in that a friend was with me that night, and had she not come to the door when she heard my screams, had she not pounded on that door as I called out to her, my experience could have been much worse. I have so much gratitude for this. It didn't matter to me if anyone knew; I didn't need to be believed by others. But she knew. She was there. She saved me.

Anyone who has ever experienced sexual assault will likely agree that there is an outrage that lives in you afterward. That outrage can create a number of responses. You can take from it bitterness and anger, you can take from it fear and resentment, or you can take from it strength. Most of the time, you move through all of it, one way or another.

Through the significant experiences of my life to that point, from my dad's alcoholism and extreme discipline to my parents' divorce to Julie's death to the sexual assault, I innately knew that I could find and take strength from the experiences—or not. I chose to find it. That's the lion in me, the *Oh Hell No* side of me. One might believe that less-than-ideal situations bring negativity into one's life, and they sometimes do, but make no mistake, I will do what I need to do in order to take the experience for my gain. That's simply the way I've responded ever since such a circumstance was first put in front of me.

The complex details of the sexual assault aren't as important to focus on as the uncomplicated fact that it happened. What matters—to me, anyway—is the way it affected me. I blamed myself for a period of time, and in a way, took responsibility for the actions of others. Before Julie's death, I'd never consumed any alcohol. All I did was go to church and school. That night, I was wearing short shorts and a half-shirt, and I was high. The police wanted me to prosecute the boys, but I thought, "I know exactly how this is going to go down. They will blame me, rip me to shreds, and I know I don't have the emotional bandwidth to handle it." (At the time, I of course didn't use phrases like "emotional bandwidth," but it well describes the way I felt). I took care of myself by forcing the night to end there. I had enough awareness to know that the decision was mine to make, and that I needed to make it *for me*. As time went on, I began to feel a level of guilt about what had happened because I felt so much shame around being high, dressed provocatively, and putting myself in a position where such a thing could happen. But one can't get to a place of resolution until she gets rid of the guilt she feels.

The main takeaway at the time was that there was no way to know for sure if I could trust a boy going forward. My trust in that portion of the population pretty much became non-existent and stayed that way for a long time. I wasn't, nor did I become, a "give them the benefit of the doubt" kind of person as a result of all of this. My low-calorie drug protocol was getting me nowhere fast, and—based on a subconscious conclusion that I had to become both daughters for the sake of my parents—I quickly made some decisions.

Julie had been a member of the National Honor Society, the Who's Who among American high school students, an artist, a dancer, a musician, and a writer. And then there was me, a girl who didn't see a fluid dram of that sort of talent in herself. I didn't believe I had a collegiate gene in my body, and I was terribly impatient. I simply didn't have time to learn what college professors thought they needed to teach me and was determined to find what I needed to learn all on my own. You could say that there's a little bit of pigheadedness in me, but overall I was nothing more or less than determined to be successful on my own terms, to be the exception to the rule, to prove wrong those who were telling me that I wasn't going to amount to anything unless I got a college degree.

The achiever in me kicked in and took over, at which point any talent that lay dormant during my youth suddenly came to life. I was determined to be the unlikely success story. Between my stubborn determination to be the exception and the belief that I needed to play the role of both daughters, I got a sudden burst of "Let's go world. It's time to find out what I've got in me." I got a job, and life went on from there.

Somewhere between 1982 and 1983, I moved to California and took a job at a clothing store called Clothestime, auditing sales for the state of Texas. It wasn't long before I realized that this job was going to drive me to drink, which was *not* low-calorie, so it wasn't going to work. I'd completely BS'd my way into the position by claiming that I knew 10-key; I absolutely did not. But I wondered, *How hard can it be?* My boss approached my desk one day and said, "You lied about knowing 10-key." My response was, "But I learned it" while wearing a sizable smile. Thank God I was likable.

Not only was the job going to drive me to drink, it wasn't going to allow me to earn what I both wanted and needed to earn, so I started looking in the newspaper for other opportunities because that's where one looked for jobs back then. I saw an opening for an assistant underwriter with an insurance company. I didn't even know what people with that title did. My mom wasn't sure I could get the job, which was precisely what I needed in order to ensure that I damn well got the job. And I did.

Insurance is a complex industry, and in order to understand it, I tirelessly educated myself. I got designations and certifications and came to realize through the process that I was inherently smarter than I'd ever realized. I was quite surprised by my innate intelligence, and being able to apply all that I was learning to different aspects of a variety of businesses was fascinating.

Once I was working in the insurance business, I wanted to advance. I was a ladder climber. The majority of salespeople in the space were men (this hasn't changed much, by the way), and I interacted with them daily. In this or nearly any other industry, you could (and can) climb the ladder or gain business by either artfully playing the female card or holding respect and being judged on your merit alone. I wanted to earn respect by doing my job well and building quality business relationships with everyone, male and female alike.

Latent feelings from Julie's passing and the sexual assault needed to be sorted out. While I'd been so unwilling to explore myself in my earlier years, I would most certainly make up for it later. One of the best things that happened in my exploration of my feelings over the loss of my sister was the acknowledgement that, while it was a loss, it was also *not* a loss. I learned that I could look at it as a situation where someone took her, or I could look at it as though I were able to *have* her for seventeen years. This realization came in my late twenties, and it was not at all popular with my parents. I was hoping they might get a different perspective, but not having yet had a child myself, I couldn't imagine their point of view.

CHAPTER 4

I met my first husband when I was twenty-four, while still working in the insurance industry in Southern California. His friend from college was marrying my friend and co-worker, and they introduced us. He subconsciously reminded me of my father in many ways, including the fact that he was an alcoholic. Whether one knows it or not, she recognizes the behavior and "energy" of an alcoholic when she was raised by it. She's even drawn to it. Until she's not. And it takes a whole lot of self-awareness to get to that point.

He was a kind, good person, but he was also very detached, mean when drunk, and thoroughly disinterested in anything that I had to say or wanted to talk about. He also had a gregarious side, and he liked to cook the way my dad liked to cook. My dad wasn't always mean when he was drunk, but he had a ferocious anger that brewed beneath the surface and was scary. I simply traded one familiar behavior for another. Everyone around me was getting married, and so that's what we did. Our son, Andrew, was born a couple of years later.

I loved everything about being pregnant. The

thought that a little being's body was growing in me had me in amazement, and feeling the movement in my body felt like this little person saying hello to me. It also compelled the deep nurturer in me to kick in. I'd instinctively rub my belly when he moved, as though I was communicating with him and loving on him before he ever came out into the world.

Towards the end of the pregnancy, the weight of this little human on my pelvis became significantly uncomfortable, so the day before he arrived, I had myself on the treadmill. Not long after that, my water broke (at the Paradise Valley Mall, no less), and seventeen hours after arriving at the hospital, Andrew Conner, arrived into the world.

We chose the name Andrew because, in the Bible, Andrew was one of the first disciples to follow Jesus. He didn't need anyone to go before him. This showed powerful courage. We chose Conner as his middle name because it sounded cool and it wasn't a common name at the time; it was unique. As it turned out, Andrew is both courageous and unique!

He had a sweetness about him, as I imagine all infants do. He had such inquisitive eyes, and looking straight into them gave me the most amazing feeling of connection I'd ever experienced. Equally magical was the feeling of him laying on my chest sleeping. I have yet to experience a superior feeling of peace.

Weeks after being born, he developed a fever of 104 degrees. We were advised to take him immediately to the hospital, where it was decided that they needed to test for spinal meningitis. This meant they would stick a needle in his spine to pull out spinal fluid. They told us that he would feel it, and when the procedure was taking place, we had to stand outside the room. Hearing his screaming cry was unbearable. As we waited to learn the results and for his fever to subside, his father returned to work and I took a quick trip to the cafeteria. When I returned to his room, there was a man sitting in a chair, holding him. I immediately went to the nurses' station and asked who this man was, holding my son. They told me it was the father, at which point I declared, "No he isn't!" and security was immediately called. They had me wait outside the room while they addressed the situation. Every minute felt like an hour. All I wanted to do was hold my child.

As it turned out, this man's child had been brought to the hospital via helicopter because he was throwing up blood. The man had even attempted to give his son mouth-to-mouth resuscitation. They explained that the distraught father was turned around and thought he was in the right room. When he saw Andrew, he thought it was his son and, feeling such a sense of relief that he "looked so good," he picked him up, sat down, and fell asleep.

That experience broke my heart, and at the same time it gave me immediate perspective. A few days later, Andrew's fever subsided, there was no sign of spinal meningitis, and we took him home.

The early challenge for Andrew (and us) was that after I stopped breastfeeding—which I did a couple of weeks after he was born, as I was pretty sure I would lose a breast from the experience—we discovered that he couldn't tolerate milk, soy, or anything else. He would projectile vomit on the regular. His little belly was so uncomfortable, and finding a solution to that became my mission.

As a young child, Andrew was an incredibly alive, magical, bright, intelligent, challenging human being who lit up my world. His mind moved so fast and his body right there with it. He was a kid who stepped into this world with abandon and sensitivities and bold awareness, which created all kinds of uncommon circumstances.

The trouble he got into in school wasn't ever about him doing something awful but about the fact that the rules—such as needing to stay in one's seat or not speak out of turn or not throw ink pens on the sidewalk—didn't make sense to him. If he felt restless, he got up. The world seemed to want to make him "wrong" for that in a way that bestowed shame upon him. Andrew had always gotten himself in trouble as a young boy because he simply didn't operate the same way other kids did. His behavior wasn't so much a matter of disrespect; it was a result of the fact that he didn't understand why the rules were what they were. Many of them didn't make sense to him. He also felt that respect was not absolutely owed just because someone was an adult, which was a thought he came by all on his own. He felt that respect should be earned. In addition, he vehemently believed that kids deserved respect as well—a point hard to argue with.

From an early age, one of the things that made him different was his inability to conform. As an extroverted introvert, he couldn't sit still in his chair, he couldn't be quiet, he couldn't *not* say something if he thought it was funny, and he was always made wrong for this by his teachers and anyone else in an authoritative position.

As you can imagine, conversations about ADHD were raised by his teachers, and it was a challenge he was eventually diagnosed with. We (meaning I) did everything possible to navigate this diagnosis without medication. I tried natural supplements, added DHA, pulled out red dyes, and tried to adjust his diet (though his interest in food revolved primarily around anything with cheese as the main ingredient). I brought in a tutor and of course tried a variety of consequences and rewards. I tried grounding him when he wasn't demonstrating preferred school behavior and rewarding him when he did. Neither the consequence nor the reward seemed to have a lasting impact.

I read books about ADHD, learned about the maturation of the frontal lobe of boys', and learned about what happens with the management function of the brain. All of this helped with my understanding, but it in no way brought a solution. I stayed with my pursuit of understanding and trying to figure out a solution right up to the point when the challenge was significantly impacting his grades. Then and only then did we try medication, and I regretted doing so because his personality changed while on them. He became subdued, not himself. It was so hard to figure out, and I had to choose to believe that, over time, it would work itself out.

I believe that many of his early challenges were, in part, a result of his wiring. Years later, when Andrew took the Gallup StrengthsFinder™ assessment, it was easy for me to see many of the puzzle pieces that were missing, contributing to a less-than-thorough understanding of my own kid. His top ten, in order, were Ideation, Adaptability, Futuristic, Strategic, Woo, Competition, Developer, Command, Communication, and Positivity. If you look up the definition and substance of each of these talents and then think about the way they work in concert with one another, things start to make more sense. Unfortunately, we don't teach from the framework of individual wiring, learning styles, or talent development.

We all have a tendency to ask ourselves on occasion, "What's wrong with me?" but that question often stems from somebody having asked us, "What's wrong with you?" The teachers couldn't figure out how to deal with Andrew because he was different and honestly disruptive to the class. One of his second-grade teachers thoughtlessly asked him, "What's wrong with you?" One of them went so far as to tell him that he was "bad," saying, "You're a bad boy." What a brilliant way to plant that fruitful seed of self-doubt in a child's head, the kind of seed that can sprout with reckless abandon.

Yes, there are rules that need to be followed and respect that needs to be demonstrated. But our education system is broken in so many ways, and this is but one example. There is an expected conformity that might be viewed as structure. Conformity, however, is not always the perfect bedfellow of structure.

But I digress.

There's beauty in coming to understand your child while trying to help him or her navigate what it's like to be in the world and loving who they are as they're growing. Of course, there were moments when I was like, "Oh, for God's sake, how can you realize this is *not* the thing to do?" But because of all of those circumstances and experiences and unbelievable energy and fast thinking, I was constantly engaging patient love.

Love first. In all things love. That's always been part of my philosophy, and it's a concept I danced with over the years. As a result, when the really hard stuff hit, I was seasoned to it. It wouldn't be until twenty-some years later when I had the following text exchange with Andrew that I'd realize, *We don't even recognize what's being built in us when it's being built.*

> Do you know, I feel like the luckiest mom in the world.
>
> *I'm the luckiest son in the world! So amazing to have you in my life to mold me as I grew. You've been so patient* [prayer hands emoji]. *I just cried tears of joy on my way to work today.*
>
> That touches my soul so much, my son. You've overcome so much and have so much to be proud of.
>
> *I am proud. I truly am. It's so amazing.*
>
> More than overcoming, you've become and continue to become such a special human being.

All through the journey that was still to unfold, he was having the experience of growing and being molded through patient love. I, on the other hand, was having an experience of recognizing what it is to *have and further develop* patient love. So hard. So fantastic.

CHAPTER 5

Patient love with life itself has both existed and been refined in me throughout my life, and certainly through raising Andrew. It most greatly evolved while going through the swamp season, and trust me when I say that I had plenty of opportunities to practice the application of it. There are threads of patient love inside each of us, and the depth to which it is experienced requires a unique level of endurance that is not always easy.

The ability to fully show up in patient love requires trust and belief that all things are going to happen as they should, and it ultimately brings understanding that there is an end to the hard things as well as a purpose. It is in the awareness and acceptance of both what we can and cannot control. It's not reflected in the habit of meekly stating, "This too shall pass." It's exposed when one can find the value and substance within a given situation. It's found through holding onto enough belief that you are able to participate in the unfolding without having a clenched-fist grip on things. It requires non-rushing. There may very well be no better application of trusting the process than the practice of patient love, especially while raising children.

Through slow and steady grasp of this concept, I am now able to see that the only way I could apply patient love was to practice a state of trust and belief, which required that I not react so much to any particular situation at hand. It required that I become a faithful observer and give both effort and intention to moving from and responding from that place. This practice is intuitive, deeply rooted, cellular. Without that component, you can't be fully in it. Neither the person you're engaging with nor yourself will, in a specific moment, fully understand what patient love truly means, feels like, and creates.

When I think about the experience of patient love with Andrew, I see that it also includes threads of a loving acceptance of where we *all* are, regardless of where that place may be. I sometimes imagine being the younger version of him, wonky and wacky, having a mom who declares what needs to be declared but who also demonstrates patient, consistent love no matter what. If I didn't have trust and belief that this was *his* journey and one that would unfold beautifully, I don't think I could have brought myself into a full state of patient love as often as I needed to.

A situation unfolding "beautifully" doesn't imply that there is an absence of ugly parts. It suggests that we embrace each aspect of it as part of a perfect whole that is refining our being during our time on Earth. Without patient love, I believe that fear would have come in much more powerfully. Judgement (in other words, fear) would have donned my doorstep with determined frequency. My attempts to control a situation would have appeared with fervor. I'm not suggesting that I didn't attempt *some* degree of any or all of those. But I had enough awareness to catch myself and realize what wasn't effective, and I believe that being present enough to know what each moment needed most saved both of us.

As Andrew got older, his sensitive, empathic nature continued to be evident and was highly affected by his relationship with his father who lay a lot of anger-laced words onto Andrew without truly having an awareness of his sensitive nature. All these factors played a part in Andrew coming into his experience, and navigating them required the employment of a tremendous amount of patience. We may be spiritual beings having a human experience, but we still have to have the human part of the experience. We create meaning around events and have attachments to things, to the way we perceive events and to the way they are presented in our lives. We're immersed in a constant dance between the human experience of "I lost my sister too early" and the spiritual experience of wondering what that means (and then realizing that it means whatever we tell ourselves it means). Simply reconciling all of that on a regular basis is a magnificent challenge—not to mention when some of this awareness begins to show up and you're only six years old.

Kids come into this world so amazingly unblemished, with a magical ability to see cleanly and purely, and oftentimes, pure brilliance comes out of their mouths. If only we could all live from that place. My best friend, Lisa, and I took Andrew to the circus once, and he sat on her lap, as a mere three-year-old, holding the sparkly light-up wand I'd bought him. Every so often, he would enthusiastically thrust the wand up into the air with both hands, holding it there for a time. I finally asked him what he was doing, and he said, "I'm taking in what I like." Lisa and I looked at each other with gobs of amazement and zero words. I didn't understand just how innately in tune he was (and, of course, he didn't know it himself, being just three years old) until that moment, during which I realized, *Holy smokes, this is gonna be an interesting road.* What a concept: taking in what you like.

Wise beyond his young years, my friends were often blown away by the awareness and insights that would come out of Andrew's young mouth. I remember the first week of first grade, specifically the afternoon when I realized just how in trouble I was with this one. He'd just come home from school, and while he ate his snack he decided to share with me his thoughts about his teacher.

"Mom," he said, "I know she is supposed to be in

charge of me, but it just doesn't seem like she is."

That little man could see *her*—not her physical body, but her substance, her confidence, her authority (or lack thereof). What a gift for a spirit having a human experience to be bestowed, and yet it became an enormous part of his struggle, because with that awareness come sensitivities and the battle to figure out where you fit in the world, which we all contend with to varying degrees. In my observation, the higher a person's ability to see intuitively, the more challenging life can be—especially when they're young.

CHAPTER 6

About five years in, my marriage with Andrew's father was not working. He was having a relationship solely with the beer that was in his hand and whatever sporting event was on television on a regular basis (at least, this is how his priorities appeared to me). We had no real connection, and I was craving both connection and companionship. I craved a relationship that, in my heart, I wanted to believe was possible, and yet the evidence in front of my face made it crystal clear that it wasn't possible with this man. I felt desperately alone in my own home.

At one point, we tried counseling, and the counselor said, "You need to get to know each other." The suggestion was made to set up a date night to hang out and talk to each other." So we did. We planned to go to dinner on a Sunday night, and I was so excited. I came into the living room, all ready to go, and he was watching the football game, not looking even a little bit ready.

I said, "This was the night we were going to spend together."

He responded, "But the game!" in his sort of charmingly funny way with an open hand gesturing toward the TV. That was the last straw for me. I stripped off my nice clothes and sank into the bathtub. While there, he came into the bathroom and tried to make light of his comment. I told him I was hanging on by a thread, a comment that he didn't seem to understand or know how to respond to.

I knew I had to either accept that this was how it was going to be for the rest of my life or believe for something better—even though I was in the midst of raising a two-year-old. I had to figure out (to some degree anyway) my own worth, and somehow claim the fact that I mattered. After all, the person who was supposed to want to know me, love me, and enjoy me (at least in my mind and heart, that's how I thought it should/could be) seemed to feel those feelings the very least.

One day when wrestling with the decision of leaving, I drove to the cemetery where my sister was buried. My parents had picked a nice area that was separated from the other headstones by a square hedge, with benches and a statue of some godly looking figure nearby. I wanted to feel close to my sister and just sit with it all and listen. In an amazing moment, I looked up in the sky and I saw one bird flying in a way that looked like a dance, and into my head came the words "Fly Free."

My entire self-identity had to be rebuilt, and I

made a commitment to God that I wouldn't get serious with anyone for several years. When I looked back at how I interacted, communicated, and behaved at that time, I saw a glaring lesson that was yet to be learned. In short, my personal communication abilities sucked! I would stuff things, ignore them and say nothing, in my attempt to be "the good wife." And then, because I didn't understand what I was really feeling or really wanted, the top of my head would blow off. I realized I had no idea how to communicate my feelings because, growing up, when my dad spoke, we listened. *We did not talk.* Retrospect helped me to see that—although it was painfully uncomfortable to acknowledge—I was also a big part of the reason for the lack of health in this relationship. After all, we were young, barely figuring out how to do life, let alone love.

Given that I didn't have a clue (and let's just forget about full awareness) of where I was on the "relationship evolution" scale, my new mission was: Personal Growth, Level One. I read books like *The Road Less Traveled* and *The Celestine Prophecy*. I attended personal growth workshops and enrolled in time management courses. I attended workshop events like The Forum (now Landmark Education). It was a time during which my focus was honed in on my growth, my son, and my career.

During this time, a dear friend gave me a beautiful and simple book that contained the poem "Desiderata." It truly spoke to me, and I've probably read it a hundred times, mostly during my more wobbly moments.

Go placidly amid the noise & haste, and remember what peace there may be in silence.
As far as possible and without surrender be on good terms with all persons.
Speak your truth quietly and clearly and listen to others, even the dull & ignorant; they too have their story.
Avoid loud and aggressive persons, they are vexatious to the spirit.
If you compare yourself to others, you may become vain or bitter; for there will always be greater and lesser persons than yourself.
Enjoy your achievements as well as your plans.
Keep interested in your own career, however humble; it is a real possession in the changing fortunes of time.
Exercise caution in your business affairs; for the world is full of trickery.
But let not this blind you to what virtue there is; many persons strive for high ideals; and everywhere life is full of heroism.
Be yourself. Especially, do not feign affection.
Neither be cynical about love; for in the face of all aridity & disenchantment it is as perennial as the grass.

Take Kindly the counsel of the years, gracefully surrendering the things of youth.
Nurture strength of spirit to shield you in sudden misfortune.
But do not distress yourself with dark imaginings.
Many fears are born of fatigue and loneliness.
Beyond a wholesome discipline, be gentle with yourself.
You are a child of the universe, no less than the trees and the stars; you have a right to be here.
And whether or not it is clear to you, no doubt the universe is unfolding as it should.
Therefore, be at peace with God, whatever you conceive Him to be.
And whatever your labors & aspirations, in the noisy confusion of life keep peace in your soul.
With all its sham, drudgery & broken dreams, it is still a beautiful world.
Be Cheerful. Strive to be happy.
—Written by Indiana poet Max Ehrmann, registered copyright 1927

I took this poetry in, over and over. It was, and still is, manna from heaven for my soul. As I wrote this just now, I am reminded of how much its words have impacted the way I have navigated life.

At first, Andrew and I lived in a one-bedroom apartment, and I decorated half the bedroom like a toddler's room in primary colors with firetrucks, school buses and stop signs on the wall. The other half was decorated like a grown woman's room. Purple was my favorite color at the time, so my side of the room boasted purple irises on the wall and the bedding. In the evening during the same weekend when Lisa came and we took Andrew to the circus, we decided to watch a kid-friendly show with him. He went into our bedroom, got his three-by-three blanket from Gymboree full of primary colors, spread it out on the floor, and was insistent that each of us lie on this blanket. It was hilarious to attempt to fit part of all three of our bodies on that little blanket. It also showed me just how strongly this incredible, developing human craved connection.

From there we moved to a two-bedroom apartment. At the same time, I had stepped from a service role into a sales role. At first glance, the new role seemed easy. I knew the business, I loved people, I had proven my ability to learn, to execute, and I wondered *How hard can it be?* The transition from service to sales is a tough one, and it challenges one's resilience over and over. Sales is a ride not unlike a roller coaster, and learning to flow with it is key to one's success in that arena. After a bit of a tumultuous start, I became successful at sales and was given the new title, Assistant VP of Sales, with Poe & Brown.

I also achieved Top Producers Club, which came with a reward trip to Florida. There was an awards dinner, and even though I wasn't at the top of the list,

I was there, and no one could take that away from me. When it was time, I walked up to the front of the room with a combination of deep gratitude and significant pride to receive my award plaque. The best part of the experience, however, was the way I took it all in. I was *living experientially.* On the day we had a decent amount of free time, I rented a bike and rode down the beach at an enjoyable pace to a private, quiet area. I went swimming, enjoyed the feeling of the sand under my feet, and let myself truly feel and celebrate where I was. I sat looking out at the beauty, smelling the salt and the sand, listening to the movement of the water, and writing in my journal. It felt like such an incredible victory, all things considered. What I wanted so badly to achieve—to be the exception to the rule—happened. What an amazing feeling that was.

My journal entry from that day:

I can't believe I am sitting here. It's so beautiful. I am so proud of myself, of the courage it took to step in, to try. What a road to this moment. I love this feeling. I want more of this feeling.

With a bit of restlessness and a desire to learn something new and challenge myself even more, I wanted to see what it would be like to leap into a new role. I left Poe & Brown to take a job with Minico as their commercial insurance division manager. Shortly after I began working for Minico, I was able to buy my own house, which provided another amazing feeling of accomplishment.

CHAPTER 7

I had started attending Christ's Church of the Valley with Andrew and decided it would be good for me to join a Bible study. I loved the church and the sense of community I felt the entire time I attended (which lasted for about fifteen years). The only bible study that interested me was one called Experiencing God. That title grabbed me because of my focus on all that comes from life's experiences.

I showed up at the host's house, where I knew no one, and had to leave early because the next morning I was flying to California to visit my stepdad, Burt, who had just undergone prostate cancer surgery. I walked out the door feeling good about having chosen this particular Bible study, and when I got to my car, I discovered that I had a flat tire. I don't change tires. It's an intentional choice. I'm a badass, but I don't change tires.

I went back into the host's house and announced my predicament. Men being men, they collectively and immediately jumped to help. I do so love this quality within them. Within three minutes, the entire Bible study was outside around my midnight blue, four-door Honda Accord, surmising what to do next.

One of them took charge. I asked him if he thought it would make it to the airport the next morning, and he asked what time I had to be there. I told him 11:00, and he said, "I'll take you and get your tire fixed while you're gone." When I got back from California, he was waiting for me at the gate with roses (this was before TSA regulations began to only allow passengers at the gate). He took me home, and we sat in my living room and talked for four hours straight. It felt a bit like a storybook romance, and I loved it.

During our first holiday season together, I remember going up an escalator in Dillard's as we did some Christmas shopping, and he said, "You don't trust me." One step above him, I responded, "Trust is hard for me." That exchange helped me realize that I needed to try to communicate and open up a bit if I were going to have the kind of relationship I truly wanted to have with a man. I became more transparent, and that was the beginning of me opening up my heart. However, I still remained slightly guarded. There was something about that particular relationship that never allowed me to feel like I could be my whole self. I had shut off the curious explorer in me and walked around in the metaphorical suit that demonstrated a life well lived.

We were married when Andrew was seven. By that point, I was, for the most part, still living with a protective wall around my heart (the wall was thinner, but it was still present). Nonetheless, he checked all the boxes, and I loved him. I love him to this day, in fact. There was something very special about our life together, and the truth is, I'll always have love for anybody I've ever felt that emotion toward. But it wasn't, in the end, a true partnership that included deep, free and open companionship (no, I am not referring to the practice of being a swinger). We were each other's "person" in some ways, but not in areas that would become glaringly apparent as vital in my life. I needed to fit into a specific mold, which didn't leave a lot of breathing room for me to explore thoughts or beliefs outside of it.

I would also add that during the majority of our life together, he traveled all week, every week for work. This lifestyle tends to be incredibly hard on a relationship. It was as if, during the week, I was a single mother while on the weekend I was a mother *and* a wife. It felt like I was living two separate lives, and we didn't have the skills or even an awareness of the need to weave those two lives together. I imagine that he felt as alone as I did, but it wasn't something we talked about. We didn't maintain a strong connection during his trips, which, in many ways, was fine for me because I was focused on life at home. There was, however, a price for that apparent ease that I didn't realize we were paying.

My relationships reflected the fact that, regardless of what I claimed to want so badly, I'd blocked off my heart by putting up an impenetrable wall between the outside world and the inner me. That wall was never their responsibility to take down; it was mine. I had not learned to practice the principle of giving and expecting whole honesty, of living from a place of "This is me and I can express from here." In previous relationships, any time I attempted to express whole honesty, I was shut down, condemned, or shut off. The notion and power of giving and expecting whole honesty was presented to me that day, to a degree, on the escalator. It eked its way into my life and grew from there, taking its first full breath of life in response to the insanity that was 2011.

That wall I kept around me did serve me, however. It enabled me to become a much more logical woman. Many of my choices over time have been less emotional. Emotions aren't a bad thing, of course, but I've learned how to marry logic and emotion very well. It's about being the leader of your thoughts and slowing yourself down enough to get clear on which thoughts you want to hold. Earlier in my life, I was far too feelings-driven. I didn't even understand that there was a way to connect my feelings with my thoughts. I often felt as though emotion were nothing more than a blue-grey sea bobbing around me without intention. As I became more logical, I began to look at my emotions as informers, and that is how I learned to use my thoughts, feelings, and actions in concert with one another. Little did I know, my logical side would play an extremely important role in the years to come, and I can, in part, thank the insurance industry experience for this found appreciation for logic.

The emotions we feel are, in large part, a response to the thoughts we are having. And for those of us whose thought machines can spin out that can result in feelings of fear, stress, anxiety, and self-doubt. There are times when we can catch our thoughts and easily re-direct them—if we are conscious enough to catch it. There are other times when the feelings take on a life of their own, and I've found that the only way to get back to center is to slow myself and marry my heart with my head. That process begins with intentional breathing. It's followed by four questions, in the following order:

- What am I thinking/feeling?
- How do I want to feel?
- What is the best possible outcome (BPO) here?
- What is the action or communication for this BPO?

We lived the life one would expect of a church-going family, attending church services most Saturday nights or Sunday mornings. We played together, rode motorcycles, attended small-group Bible studies, and shared in friendships with some incredibly beautiful souls whom I love deeply. I adored this season of life. But there was also always an underlying current of disconnection, of separation, of aloneness. There was curiosity about what was happening in the life he was living, and just as important, there was part of an unexpressed, curious explorer in me brewing, wanting to rise to the surface.

In May 2000, I retired my insurance career. When you're a ladder climber (and I was), in order to continue and thrive in certain roles it's beneficial to be driven by money or power. I was driven by neither. I was realizing that I wanted to live more experientially and deeply explore myself. On the day I left, as I had done prior to leaving my first marriage, I needed to connect with myself first. I walked to the back of the office building where there was a balcony, my typed resignation in my hand. As I stood on the balcony I looked up to the sky. On my mind and heart was the question, *Is this the right decision?* I saw a tall flagpole in the distance, the risen flag resting comfortably against the pole. I thought, *If this is the right decision, move that flag*. I kid you not, the flag began to move, to flow, to wave. Without a second thought, I turned around, walked straight into the president's office, and resigned.

Andrew was eight at this point, and my newfound love genuinely wanted me to be able to explore who I really was, underneath all the layers that had built up around me over time. Just because we didn't have the kind of partnership I craved doesn't mean he wasn't an amazing person. Encouraged by him, I enrolled in our local community college to study photography and learn to work in a darkroom. It seemed to be a good way to explore creativity in an area that had a certain intellectual component to it, but it was someone else's idea.

The first subtle sign of the perilous passage that would ensue years later occurred during our tuck-in routine one night when Andrew was about Nine. After we said prayers, Andrew told me he was scared because he knew that in the future he was going to give in to temptation. The way he posed his trepidation made me realize that he was referring to something significant. I held my countenance (even though it concerned me) and told him that God always provides a way out. When I think back to this little boy's premonition, it still gives me chills.

CHAPTER 8

When Andrew was sixteen, he ran away. My husband was gone on business, and as I headed to bed one night after turning off the kitchen lights, I could see him down the hallway as I walked to my own room. He was looking out the door with an expression on his face that caused me to think, *Something's up with him.* It wasn't anything I could properly assess in the moment, but the next morning I woke up, and his bedroom door was closed. The minute I saw that closed door, I knew something was wrong. He never closed his bedroom door. I opened the door, saw that the window was open, and realized that he was gone.

He had left a note that said something to the effect of "Don't come looking for me." At some point over the previous few years, I'd mentioned to him that I would hunt him down if he ever did something like that. And that is exactly what happened.

There truly hadn't been any strong indication that something like this was on the horizon. He was on the swim team and having some conflicts with the new coach, but I thought the coach was an asshole, so I didn't give those conflicts much thought. He was starting to do things with friends more often, whereas before he was more focused on spending time with his family. I was observant of who he was hanging out with, but at the same time, I didn't know all of his friends. He had also become resistant to going to church with us. I thought all of it was normal behavior for a teenager.

My mind was reeling in fifteen directions at once. *What happened? Why did he do this? Where did he go? When did he leave? Who is he with? What is wrong? What have I been missing? What if he is hurt? How do I find him? Why would he do this to me? The better question is,*

What is happening inside of him that would cause him to do this? And, with that, I fell to my knees in prayer.

There was one kid he was hanging out with a lot, and I knew in my gut that I needed to keep my eyes on the situation and pay close attention. I knew generally where this kid lived, and through what I can only assume was a mother's intuition, I knew that's where Andrew was—or at least had an extremely strong feeling that he was there.

I paused just long enough to ponder the possibility that he was having a hard time and wanted some space to get his head together. I thought, *Don't find him. Let him do what he needs to do*, but that thought didn't last long. I called both the police and Andrew's father, who came over as quickly as he could, but by the time he arrived, the police had come and gone. They had gotten the information they needed and proceeded to head to Andrew's school. I said, "I don't know where he is, but there is a kid he's been hanging around," and told him the general direction in which said kid lived.

Andrew's father began driving around that area and found Andrew's truck parked in front of a house. He knocked on the door and told the kid who answered to go get Andrew, who was, by that point, high as a kite. This was the first time I knew that he had ever smoked marijuana. It was the first time I knew he was doing *anything* like this. They came back to the house, and I told him to go to his room. We let the police know that we found him and waited to begin the "What the hell are you doing?" conversation until he woke up the next morning and was sober. Andrew's father was my hero through that entire experience.

The story Andrew told was that he wasn't getting high often. It was exactly the explanation you'd expect to hear, and while I knew there was a problem, I wasn't quite sure how to navigate it. We took his truck keys and told him we didn't want him hanging around those friends anymore—they clearly weren't a good influence on him. He would have to earn back our trust. Unfortunately, the situation only escalated from there.

In the coming months, my husband and I would

try to get him to go to Teen Challenge, which is a program for anybody who is struggling with addiction, although the majority of its participants are teenagers. The program is religion-based, founded on the fundamentals of Christianity, and the recovery belief is that the solution is a right relationship with God.

It's critical to note that I have a deeply rooted faith. In my life, spiritual openness is an absolute requirement. I was raised Methodist and became a born-again Christian when I was in seventh grade. From that point, I went from Nazarene to a non-denominational Bible-based church with Jesus as the example of teacher and savior. As time went on, I had large seasons of my life that revolved around church. And something about that always felt right and yet a tiny bit off. It wasn't that the core beliefs or even the teachings of the Bible felt wrong. It wasn't that I am not crazy in love with Jesus and all that he was and is; I am. His example is an extraordinary one. It was more that the "religious" framework around those beliefs and teachings were ones that I did and still do struggle with. It's not about the religious framework, about who's framework is right or wrong. It's about the essence, the meaning, the common thread of truth. Your rules want you to be right; they want there to be one right answer. And yet the fact is, no one knows with one hundred percent certainty what parts are absolutely true and what parts are our human mind's additions to the spiritual aspect of living.

I believe in something so much greater than myself. I believe that there is a human evolution that is God inspired, and that is a piece of how I've been able to navigate. I've claimed and held onto that and without that, I don't know that my steps would have been the same. Our desire to be right is part of what's screwing up our world. Your religious beliefs and framework are *for you.* You get to choose them. But you don't get to demand of me that I choose what you do, and you don't get to make me wrong for it either.

Before Andrew's big troubles started, when I was in the season of my life when I was regularly attending church, I was scheduled to attend a local Christian business conference. I was intrigued by how they would apply Christian principles to business. The morning of Day One of the conference, Andrew and I had an argument, and I was very frustrated that I wasn't going to be on time. As I walked into the building, the conference had already started. A woman was still in the hallway after ushering participants into the main meeting room. I apologized for being late, and for some reason, revealed that I'd had a struggle with my son.

She said, "A few minutes ago I wondered why I was still out here" and then shared the story of her daughter and the challenges they were experiencing based on regular teenage antics.

"I'm going to give you a scripture," she said,

which essentially proclaimed *Your children will come home.* In that moment, my only thought was *Holy Shit.* I know, probably not the best combination of words given the topic, but it was what I thought, nonetheless. Prayer—communion with all that is—has been and continues to be a huge part of my life, and I believe with every fiber of my being that I was given that scripture because what I was about to go through was going to be one heck of a ride, and I needed to claim the truth that everything was going to be okay. Over the following months and years, I would refer back to that scripture many times to let go of the leaf of worry and, with the same hand, grab the branch of hope. This is how the godly universe interacts with us. In tiny moments like this. To miss that, we cheat ourselves out of the value of divinity, the substance, the gift that those moments bring to us.

We took him to a "Come Learn About Teen Challenge" day, and suffice it to say, he was *not* on board. He thought it was stupid and completely ridiculous that he was there at all. He only went because we made him go, and he made it clear that he had no intention of ever attending that program. Yes, we could have forced him to go—he was seventeen and young enough for us to do that—but I was keenly aware that forcing him would backfire at that point. I had researched a number of different programs (including the kind where a group is sent to make their way in the desert for a few weeks), but none of them felt "right." Combine Andrew's reluctance with my uneasiness about which program was the best fit and the fact that my dad was having all kinds of challenges by that point—there were many days when I'd find him heavily intoxicated or debilitatingly hungover—and it seemed that perhaps this just wasn't the right time to put Andrew into a program.

Desperate to help him and keep him busy doing healthy things, I helped Andrew find jobs instead of requiring him to find them himself. I tried to let him find them on his own, but he had little interest in giving real effort to that. Given that I knew he needed the job as a distraction, I took action instead. I would literally find him the job and help him apply. All he had to do was go in and sell himself, and he of course got the job every time because that's who Andrew is. In no time, however, he'd be let go, and I'd be off to find him a new opportunity.

Newsflash: When people use drugs, they need money to buy those drugs. If they can't keep a job and aren't being given money, they start to steal. My husband noticed that money and sellable items were going missing from our house, but Andrew was—as he'd always been—extraordinarily convincing that he wasn't the guilty party. Still, there was a part of me that knew he wasn't telling the truth. Even still, it was as though I simultaneously couldn't accept the possibility of that. It was too much to consider that my child would be stealing from us.

Andrew continued to spend time with kids who seemingly wanted to live in a world that was not good for Andrew (or themselves). I knew I was in the dance between "I can't control what you do outside of the house, and I also can't lock you in your room" and "How do I put restrictions on you? At what point are those restrictions ineffective? What do I do to maintain communication?" I wondered how to shut his behavior down while at the same time keep my arms around the situation to any small degree. The spin-out ensuing in my head held nearly equal power to my determination to be grounded and aware of the present-moment opportunity. Let me tell you, that shit was exhausting!

To help give you a sense of where in the timeline this all was occurring, at this point in the adventure my dad was still alive, and I'd essentially taken over the day-to-day logistics for both Andrew and him. In addition, my husband had lost his job, and although he'd gotten a new one, his income level wasn't where we needed it to be in order to comfortably pay the bills. While all that was happening at home, Andrew was getting into more trouble. The calamitous storm that was mounting was becoming more and more clear, and our collective stress was escalating.

He'd disappear and sometimes return with a mysterious bruise on his face. It was fairly traumatic for me (especially as someone so appalled by violence), and yet I fought so hard to hold my countenance, not to lose my balance, not to overreact—though I definitely didn't succeed in that attempt at all times. There were most assuredly moments during which I reacted—strongly—but I really struggled with the balance between keeping the lines of communication open and paying attention to where my opportunities were to purposefully step in.

That whole period of time was unbelievably tough to navigate, and in hindsight, I don't know that I did any or all of it correctly, but I also truly don't know that I could have done anything differently. I think that, at that time, I was probably behaving as more of a friend to Andrew than a parent, and that led me to doing all the things that one does as an enabler.

One of those "not my best parenting moments" came when Andrew asked me if he could have some friends over for pizza and a swim in our backyard pool. The next thing I knew, a bunch of people were traveling like a line of termites from the front door to the backyard. I remember one person in particular who had a very disrespectful energy about him. I didn't like it, and there was no one home but me.

So there they were, swimming in the backyard (and, as it turned out, drinking), and there I was, sitting alone on my couch, hating every moment of it and beating myself inside up for saying yes to this get-together. I didn't want to embarrass my son in front of his friends, and yet, I wanted it to be over. A few hours went by, and at a certain point I had just had enough and told Andrew that his friends had to leave. Thankfully, he saw my resolve and didn't put up much of a fight.

I had to acknowledge to myself that, in my own way, I was an enabler. I had to get real with that, and then make different decisions. That didn't happen overnight. Some of the decisions I would soon have to make where Andrew was concerned were extraordinarily brutal, and yet they were necessary. They would have to come from a place of strength, and it's often hardest to summon that strength when you're working to build it at the same time.

With Andrew, part of my enabling behavior was born from the seeds of growing up with an alcoholic father. Another part from the natural transition most mothers seem to go through at some point when their kids are in their teenage years. Up until that point, I had always been the person who figured everything out for him. When he was younger, I was extremely excited when he came home with school projects. Once, we made a two-story replica of a portion of a mystery book. He did a lot of it on his own, and he's done some amazingly creative things, but there were certain projects that I felt compelled to help with, given the fact that, while he had two weeks to complete the project, he made no mention of it until two nights before it was due. I understand now that I wasn't alone in the hell that was created from a child's lackadaisical attitude toward due dates, and that awareness is surprisingly low in terms of its ability to provide me with a sense of hindsight camaraderie. We got a box, made levels on the inside, and created it to look like a cave using clay. He was so proud when he walked into school. And then the teacher said, "Your mom helped you here, right?" He hadn't asked me for help, per se, but he only had two days to finish the project.

There's a transition that moms go through, from "you need me" to "I want you to be independent" wherein we can miss the boat (or forget about the boat entirely). Our job as parents is to equip our children to be independent. Especially as they begin to individualize. But oftentimes, part of our identity lies in helping them. I identified as a mother, but I also identified as someone who solved problems. I was the go-to, and not just for Andrew and my dad but also for the rest of my family. The fact was, I was solving problems for him especially at the point when he needed to be solving them for himself.

When faced with what I perceived to be a crisis, I couldn't let him fail. This would be Part Three in terms of where this enabling behavior originated. It all went back to my childhood—an over-eager "let me come to your rescue" disposition that was ingrained in me at an early age. I had been so afraid of failing and was raised with a sense that I needed to strive for perfection at all times.

I remember Andrew's father once telling me when

Andrew was in elementary school that we needed to let him fail, and I thought it was the most horrendous thing that anybody could ever say. Yet he was so right. My belief stemmed from the ramifications I had wrapped around the word failure, not the ramifications my son did. A maximizer is one of the talents on the Gallup StrengthsFinder™ assessment, and it reflects someone who is driven to take something from good to great. It's the quality of being driven to excellence, which is both an innate quality of mine as well as one that was further rooted into me when I was a child. That is why I had to take some of his school projects to the *nth* degree. Good isn't good enough; my mind would instinctively move to "How can we make it great?" There is no mediocre. In fact, I loathe mediocre. This is how I'm wired, and it's both a blessing and a curse. As misguided as it was, I believed that I couldn't let failure happen to my son. That in letting failure happen to him, I was allowing it to happen to me by extension. And that had been unacceptable since the moment I took my first breath.

Shortly thereafter, my dad got sicker. My uncle was doing okay but not terribly well, and we were trying to keep all of the proverbial plates spinning. Andrew was a senior, and I felt like I was just barely keeping my hands on everything, doing my best to run the household with no idea where things with Andrew were going. I was in and out of the doctor's office with my dad, never knowing from one day to the next whether I'd get him after a binge-drinking experience, which came with some ugly moments I've never before shared. Imagine having to clean up shit from the kitchen to the living room carpet because your dad passed out drunk and lost all bowel control. Yes, that happened, and not just once.

There I was, sandwiched between these two people I loved so very deeply, both living their lives in addiction. I felt suffocated, petrified, compressed, and panicked through every cell in my body.

My son would describe my approach at that time as caretaker codependent. There's an almost indescribable unsettledness that exists within an addict—a lack of being grounded, a state of subtle internal disturbance. Whether or not you pick up on it likely depends upon how intuitive you are, and of course, whether or not it's ever before been a part of your world, but it was something I could sense from a young age, even though I didn't know what it was early on.

Those who grew up as a child of an alcoholic often bear several traits. Part of my struggle to trust and engage in true intimacy is a direct result of being the child of an alcoholic. For a very big part of my life, I put the needs of others before my own. I thrived on being the go-to person within my family and circle of friends. There was a subconscious attraction to those that needed help. I often thought, "I can help. I can counterbalance this. I see a need for me here." The psychological desire behind that enabling behavior is the need to be needed. All of us need to be needed, but when you're the child of an alcoholic, that need tends to manifest in unhealthy ways.

When my *own* child then became an addict, I subconsciously felt like I needed to be *his* protector, help him solve his problems, rescue him. As a young girl, I knew all the good that was in my father; he unfortunately didn't give credit to any of the good that he saw in himself (if he saw any at all). I wasn't so much interested in fixing things for him as I was in helping him see things differently so he could live a better life. In the end, he had a different mechanism when it came to processing life situations. Changing or fixing that wasn't my job. I finally accepted this truth during a visit with my uncle while in San Diego—he was the one who helped me let it go.

In the middle of all of this chaos, on a day I visited my father, I stood with him in his one-bedroom condo as he proceeded to melt down in apology. "I'm sorry" was repeated over and over while he sobbed, and I just hugged him and told him, "I forgive you." The thing is, I wasn't all too sure what I was forgiving him *for*. It could have been his guilt over everything, over his alcoholism and what comes as a result of that addiction. It creates a very chaotic environment to grow up in and a very hard reality to contend with all of your life. But I will tell you, and this is also something I have never before shared, that moment disturbed me. It felt deep, and I had a sense that I didn't want to know what he was apologizing for. I didn't ask, and I will never know exactly what the answer is. What was more important to me in that moment than understanding—what I felt he most needed—was to feel forgiven.

CHAPTER 9

Nine zeros. That was the phone number from which I received a call in the middle of the night. I was almost afraid to answer, and as suspected, it was the police. They had Andrew pulled over on the side of the road, and the officer suggested that I come to where they were.

Andrew had been driving under the influence, and because of how open and respectful he was with those officers, they let me take him home after saying, "He's a good kid." He should have gotten a DUI, and I knew it, but I couldn't bring myself to encourage that to happen, nor did the officers seem interested in taking it there.

When we got home that night, I knew it was pointless to have a conversation. My son was intoxicated, and it was therefore pointless to yell, blame, or react. Honestly, in that moment, I didn't know how to respond, so I just told him to go to bed. Knowing that he was stealing *and* continuing to make poor choices, we told Andrew that we could no longer trust him, and he wasn't able to live in the house any longer. He had to live in the backyard for several weeks. We had an outdoor kitchen where he could brush his teeth, and he could come into the house to take a shower. I was in full anxiety over this approach. By the way, if you know your kid is stealing from you, don't attempt this approach. As I learned in later years, all Andrew did was have his friends over to camp out with him in the backyard and party in his tent.

For a long time, I wondered about Andrew's perspective on this "tent lifestyle" as well as on the evening when he was arrested in front of me. I wondered if he felt that being relegated to a tent lifestyle was an effective consequence. I wondered if he felt supported or felt something else altogether. So I recently asked him, and here is what he said:

I couldn't live in the house any longer because I was stealing. I now joke with my mom about how dumb her choice to move me to the backyard was at the time. She essentially gave me my own single-bedroom apartment, and I could do whatever the fuck I wanted. There was a mini fridge connected to the barbeque; I could jump in the pool each day instead of showering. I was living the drifter life, coming home whenever I wanted to. It was great. She single-handedly gave me all of the freedom I desired.

[Regarding the nearly missed DUI]
I was 17, and it was [the night of] my graduation, but I'd been kicked out of school. I was partying with my

friends who were graduating. We went from one party to another party in my friend's car. I thought my friend was going to drive; he was under the impression that I was going to drive. We both got wasted. Cops crashed the party and I ended up driving. I ran three red lights and two stop signs and was speeding. A sheriff was following me the entire time and pulled us over. The minute I pulled over, three additional sheriff cars pulled up and surrounded us.

My mom was woken up at 1:00 or 2:00am, and I remember that they said, "Listen, son, we don't want to do this, but we can either take you to jail or call your mom." I said, "Take me to jail."

My phone was dead at the time anyway.

They tried to talk me into calling my mom, but I said I didn't know my mom's number. I didn't want my mom to have any idea what had happened, I wanted to go to jail, be released and then say to her, "Sorry, I ended up spending the night at a friend's house."

They eventually convinced me to call my mom. She arrived and saw me handcuffed in the back of my friend's car, a car (and a friend) she had never seen, my friend puking on the side of the road, and five or so squad cars surrounding us.

I was so drunk that I barely knew how to care.

What I did know, even in that state, was that I was more worried about disappointing my mom than anything that could happen to me in jail.

When she arrived and saw me and I saw her, there was a level of guilt wherein there's nothing you can even say. There was no point in apologizing. She handled it like a champion; she said, "Don't worry; we'll handle it when you're sober." She took me home (along with my $500 ticket for all my traffic violations), tucked me into bed, and that was that.

CHAPTER 10

I found myself in a battle of sorts. I knew I had to keep my arms around the situation with Andrew, but not so tightly that I did more harm than good. I simply didn't know what to do, having never before been in a position like that. I certainly didn't want it to get worse, and at the same time I was trying to honor myself and ask, "Where's the lesson in this for him and for me?" That battle dance is an ever-present experience when you're in the middle of something like this. I had enough awareness to know that I both didn't have control and had to trust in the overall journey. I had enough awareness to have respect for the fact that it could all go the wrong way. I had enough awareness to understand that this was Andrew's journey as well as mine. And I had enough awareness to understand that I deserved honor and self-love through the experience. And at the same time, I was scared shitless.

I both wanted to and couldn't consistently make myself the priority. Life had become a constant question of "What does *this moment* need?" which has been a prevalent question for me throughout my life and is a way that I clear the chaos in order to know what step needs to be taken. Or not. This question is a component of practicing presence and living within patient love. It's an incredibly grounding question to ask oneself in a frantic moment. It has helped slow me down enough to get perspective. The truth was, some moments needed my full attention to be on my father, and some moments needed my full attention to be on my son, and some moments needed my full attention to be in prayer. Knowing where one's full attention needs to be in any given moment is a by-product of practicing presence—and an extremely beneficial one.

During the holiday season of 2009, we invited my father over for holiday dinner, and he showed up drunk. We handled it by making light of it via our facial expressions during dinner, but I was mortified and so disappointed that my father showed up this way. I knew this example was the last thing my son needed to see. After dinner, my father went outside to smoke a cigarette, and we went outside with him, a bit concerned about his state of intoxication. For some odd reason, he walked out into the middle of the street, took a long drag of his cigarette in an almost defiant way, and then passed out, falling backwards, his head bouncing off the concrete. Andrew watched this happen, as my emotions ping-ponged between anger, humiliation, and deep sadness.

Just prior to the end of 2010, as my father and uncle were nearing the ends of their lives, Andrew's behavioral change was taking firm hold. While he'd been struggling heavily, I didn't really realize just *how* heavily at the time because I was so busy continually rescuing my dad.

It was between Christmas 2010 and the beginning of March 2011 when Andrew was arrested on three separate occasions for possession of marijuana. There were six felony counts against him, two for each of the three cases. The attorney we hired to represent Andrew had to consolidate the six felony counts, and then we had to go to court for each one. He was another of many blessings I saw as having been delivered directly by God through this odyssey. We knew him from our small group Bible study, and he came to our aid without question.

In May 2011, they gave Andrew his sentence of probation for two years (it may have been three) along with a fine. We may have been in court only six or seven times, but it felt like one hundred. Shortly thereafter, difficult financial discussions commenced when it was revealed how much credit card debt we had. That, coupled with being completely upside down on our home, made it perfectly clear that we had to file for bankruptcy.

I knew that I had my own credit card balance, and I was aware that we were collectively in debt to some degree. However, there was debt that had been incurred, debt I didn't know about. He had a habit of transferring credit card balances and making minimum payments and not telling me about it when it was happening. There was more than one time when we had to use annual compensation bonuses to pay off multiple credit card balances simultaneously because the balances had grown so significantly. The timing of it all was what blew the lid off of the coffin containing the perfect storm.

In July we went to bankruptcy court, and our bankruptcy was finalized. Put simply, bankruptcy court is unpleasant and embarrassing, but thankfully the judge was incredibly kind. My dad had left to me his rights to our family's oil property, which represented some portion of our retirement savings plan, and I surrendered them to the court. In an instant, they were gone, and rightfully so. Part of me was happy to hand that over. It felt horrible to be there at all.

I had to find the three of us a place to live, and because we'd declared bankruptcy, we no longer had a full house of furniture. I'd had excellent credit all my life, and now it was ruined. But I refused to be a victim; I owned my reality. I could have stayed in a blaming mindset, but I hadn't asked the right questions in order to properly stay on top of our financial position. We didn't communicate about money often, and I never saw his credit card statements. I didn't even ask; I felt like that was being invasive. There was a moodiness that happened from time to time, sometimes at the dinner table, sometimes in inconsequential conversation, so I avoided that topic. That is on me. My father displayed this same moodiness growing up; you never knew who was going to be at the table, so to speak. And, as I said, I had my own credit card balance. Nonetheless, it was happening, and it felt awful.

We moved in August to a house we rented in Glendale, Arizona. We were bankrupt, our marriage was in big trouble, Andrew was spiraling, and 2011 was officially primed to be my life's raging, relentless tsunami.

Between the end of August and the beginning of January, Andrew went from being manageable to being completely *un*manageable. I didn't know who he was anymore. He'd become completely combative and extraordinarily mean. He'd say horrendous things, and I could tell he was out of his mind, but I didn't know how to navigate it. At that point, we were living together completely dysfunctionally, and believe it or not, part of my saving grace appeared in the form of a man wearing a green unitard.

CHAPTER 11

In the midst of everything else that had been uncontrollably swirling around me, I knew I needed to go after something really big. I found myself in a place where I couldn't connect to my husband, I was losing my son, I had lost my father and uncle, I had lost my home, and I'd been stripped bare financially. I didn't know what to do about any of it, and I soon recognized that I needed to cling to something that would require all of me. I didn't need a run-of-the-mill pattern interruption. I needed an absolute pattern disruption.

I wondered, *What am I most afraid of?* For most of my life, remember, I'd been a dip-your-toe-in-the-water girl, but I somehow instinctively knew that I needed to take on something really significant; I needed something that took enormous courage to conquer.

I'd always been afraid of being in front of groups. I once sang with a vocal group at church, and I ended up being asked to sing as part of a small group. I literally had to wear sunglasses while performing. You might think this happened to me as a child. It didn't. I was a grown-ass adult, and my resistance to this seemingly simple activity really freaked me out.

It's easy to let the dark veil overtake, and it sometimes feels like you have to fight to get to the light when deep darkness presents itself. There are a number of things that can bring a sense of darkness at different degrees. I had to purposely find something to hold my attention and move me toward something that felt like light. I had the sense that I needed to go after something that was big enough and had a significantly positive outcome.

So, in October 2011, I joined Toastmasters. I remember the date because I'd been visiting different clubs to find the best one, the one that would force me to stretch the most. This was my second meeting at this particular club, and it required a fifteen or so mile drive to get there. The meeting was Halloween-themed, which I had no clue about in advance, nor was I prepared for the fact that a collection of high-level executives from Scottsdale would show up in costume. The first person I saw when I walked in the door was a tall, lean man wearing a green unitard. My first thought: *What. The. Fuck.* As you can imagine, a unitard on a man is quite revealing, and it caused me not only a modicum of discomfort but also a moment in which I re-thought my club selection. Yet, by the end of that meeting, I was officially signed up as a member of the CHATS Toastmasters club, and these people would soon feel like family.

Conquering one of my biggest fears was my first big pivot, and it had many catapulting benefits in addition to serving as a form of therapy for me. In my icebreaker speech, which I gave in December, I introduced myself as someone who had decided that I needed to fully and experientially live my life as a result of my sister's death. I titled the speech "I choose to live."

The greatest gift that came from the loss of my sister was the realization that I needed to live fully, which meant that I had to step outside my comfort zone. And at the point when I was a mere shell of a woman with little-to-no clear direction, what better time to start?

There's often a gap—sometimes a big one—between the realization that you *want* to live experientially and the actual going-after of the experiences that tap into your soul and connect you to the things that hold your interest. My interests and someone else's interests of course may not be the same, but regardless, living experientially means being in full pursuit of whatever thing gives you that feeling. And yet, at the time, I didn't have any idea what that thing was.

One might wonder how living experientially is different from practicing presence. When practicing presence, I may or may not be having an experience that relates to something I want to pursue in my life, but regardless, I'm practicing presence while I'm engaged with the activity, washing dishes perhaps. Let the gift of your senses transport you. Connect to your hands, holding the glass in the warm sudsy water. Look at the color, the shape, the thickness of the glass. Let your hands splash in the water and take in the clean scent. When you do that, you will feel a greater connection to your moment and to yourself. Practicing presence is bringing yourself fully into the moment you are in. In this life we are too quick to move to the execution of the task, and in doing so, we miss so much.

Living experientially, however, is not just about going to work and coming home and doing the things and cooking dinner and washing the dishes and being present through it all. It's about really exploring one's inner being and coming to understand his or her driving passions, the things she wants to learn, the things that make him or her feel the most alive and intentionally bringing that into your world.

Bathing in the experiences that come throughout the journey are what living experientially is all about. It's about trying new things, expanding your capacity, embarking upon your dreams. It's about throwing yourself in the river and being willing to ride the currents, to see how you respond and how you become as a result of it. It's remembering that these experiences are proving grounds for our refinement. What we choose to take with us as we journey on is what matters most.

Over time and through conscious exploration, I discovered that I wanted my ass in a kayak. I discovered that I love climbing mountains. I feel closest to God when I'm alone in nature. That I love the feeling of sweating profusely during yoga. That I love taste. That I love every form of chocolate known to man. That I love wine, fruit, and color. That I love laughing with my friends. That I love sex. That I do *not* love lima beans. That I love feeling the rain on my skin.

I tried mountain biking, and I didn't love that because there was a little too much of a sense of not being able to control my destiny. I was more than a little afraid of face-planting on a rock, but I gave it a shot because I knew that it was so important that I be in full exploration of what lights my fire. That's what living experientially is all about, whereas practicing presence is about doing so regardless of the moment you're in. You're wherever you are—you aren't thinking about a conversation, futurizing, or ruminating on the past—you could be in a bathtub or sitting on your bed in conversation with a friend or paddling on a lake. Wherever you are and whatever you're doing, you're practicing presence all the while. The practice of presence as well as relishing in the experiences that I'd learned fed my soul were both about to become extremely important skills.

CHAPTER 12

You don't try heroin just one time. Once it's in your system, your body begins to crave it. And then, right before your eyes, you're into the addiction of it, and the battle has begun.

Interestingly, Andrew and I were still having connected conversations about his challenges at this point. We actively *talked* about the situation. No one's head was buried in the sand. And yet, he continued with all of the lying, and I was constantly stuck between wondering whether or not he was telling me the truth. I wanted to believe him, and I was also coming to the realization that I had unknowingly been playing my own role in his struggle. If you're willing to be aware enough, there comes a point in time where you can see the part you're playing or have played in every situation and interaction, good or bad or somewhere in between. You serve yourself and others best when you can come from whole honesty with yourself first, and doing that sometimes comes with having to acknowledge and own some uncomfortable truths.

I gave this kid a beautiful space to just sit and get high, and that fact made me culpable. At first, of course, I didn't realize I was doing that, and once I did realize it, I was too busy trying to convince myself it wasn't happening to do things differently. Then, I realized *exactly* what I was doing and was terrified of the potential outcome. It was some serious life and death shit we were dealing with! I was afraid to take action, and yet I knew that if I were to take action, I needed to be confident in which action would bring about the best possible outcome. It was time for me to start making much tougher choices.

He spent his evenings in his room behind a closed door while I was spinning out in my head about what he was or wasn't doing. I hated that feeling of anxiety—a feeling that couldn't quite be calmed because the stakes constantly felt so high.

Holding belief that the soul you know still lives in a human being you struggle to recognize is incredibly challenging. And yet, so is *not* holding belief—as a form of burying your head in the sand or diluting your thoughts in some sort of effort to cope. By holding belief, I'm referring to staying in and accepting the reality of the now while believing for the possibility of something very different. It is terribly hard to do this, because each time a situation occurs that wants to prove that you are wrong, you have to be resolved to never let your belief go, or you will invariably experience the pain that comes from the deep disappointment of a potentially unrealized life. As the mother or father, we are likely the only one still fighting to believe.

It's incredibly hard to feel others' judgement of your child, who is struggling with addiction, especially when it comes from your family. People so often judge the person and not the act. It's the easier choice. And, while it's understandable and even makes sense, it slices and makes you want to isolate. It leaves you feeling wildly alone.

I was cleaning the kitchen one evening in November, thinking about how strange it was to feel like everything was so heavy and yet concurrently feeling so numb.

I smelled something strange; it reminded me of burned sugar. His closed bedroom door combined with the odd smell made me even more suspicious of what he was doing. I knew the smell wasn't marijuana, so I went outside and walked around to his bedroom window. He was getting much skinnier, and I could see him through the window blinds, wearing a T-shirt and jeans that were so loose on him. He was just sitting there on his bed, in his own world, so completely comfortable.

Andrew had told me that some of his friends had done heroin, and for the record, when kids start talking about what other people in their circle are doing, there's a really good chance they're participating in that behavior. My Spidey sense was constantly analyzing, asking, and confronting, yet getting bullshit responses in return.

As Andrew had explained it (in regard to his friends' new habit), one way to smoke heroin is to take the ink cartridge out of a pen and put the heroin on top of a piece of aluminum foil. You then light the underside of the foil and breathe in the smoke through the empty pen. Empty pen cartridges, random pieces of aluminum foil, and black soot on someone's clothes or body renders it highly likely that they're smoking heroin. In that moment, it hit me square in the face: *Oh my God, this is really happening. My son is doing heroin.*

I was crushed. Feeling shocked, nauseous, and numb, I went back inside, knocked on his door, and calmly said, "I know what you're doing; open the door." I was so grateful for the relationship I had built with this boy up to that point, because it's what allowed the door to be opened. Of course, he made promises that he wasn't going to do it again. I didn't buy his words and started trying to figure out the next possible path. Again, my mind was assessing, "What does this moment need?" I needed some time to figure out the next move.

To further complicate matters, it was becoming more and more apparent that things in my marriage were continuing to head in the wrong direction. As good of a person as he was and is, for the majority of the marriage, I didn't feel like I had a partner who was helping me manage the day-to-day life situations, tasks, and responsibilities. I believe that, in his heart of hearts, he would have loved to have been able to affect a positive change for Andrew, and to save our marriage but I don't think he was equipped to do so. And *I* wasn't equipped to figure out how to make the marriage work.

We were married for a total of eleven years, and it was only during the final few that things were so rocky. It would be easy to blame that rockiness on Andrew's addiction, but I've taken the necessary time to explore that. While Andrew's addiction certainly added stress, it wasn't the root of the problem. The previous years felt like good years, but the truth was that I wasn't fully connected to *myself* during any of it. When we met, I was in the season of my life when I was faithfully attending church. Our marriage fit the perfect mold in terms of how I thought a good relationship *should* look and how a good life *should* be lived. While it may not have appeared from the outside as though I was alone, I felt very much alone. I had a circle of friends from church, and we called ourselves "naked," as in a certain degree of authenticity. I didn't realize it then, but I wasn't truly naked, because there were things I didn't share with anyone. I didn't feel that deep a level of comfort.

As much as my husband tried to talk to me, I felt dead inside, and we didn't have the foundation necessary for me to be comfortable exploring the topic that my son was now doing heroin. I felt like I had no one. Don't get me wrong, I did have friends I could talk to, but I could only take those conversations so far, I could only go so deep. I held back the details and the depth of what was hurting me the most. I considered leaving the environment altogether, and while I knew that if I left, I'd be leaving Andrew there, half of me felt as though that was something Andrew actually needed, as crazy as that might sound.

From there, the promises of "I won't do it again" from Andrew were constant and unending. He couldn't keep a job. He'd gotten (and lost) at least four jobs in the previous year and a half. And of course, each time he lost a job, I'd tried to help him find another one. Most of the time, one doesn't recognize that she's participating in enabling behaviors while she's doing it; hindsight can really light things up in a way that kicks your ass. The snowball had already rolled halfway down an enormous hill. And it's extremely hard to stop something that big.

At some point prior to December 2011 when we were really in the thick of things, Andrew had been missing and wouldn't answer his phone. Desperate to find him, I drove around and around. While I was headed down 67th Avenue in Glendale, we finally connected. While talking to Andrew on the phone, I admitted, "I hope I don't make it home." He claims this to be one of the two lowest moments of his life; I'll talk about the other later.

I kept thinking about how easily I could just drive my car into something and end the insanity. I couldn't figure out how to help him, and my own life was at the tail end of imploding. I felt such an enormous sense of confused shame. I was, for the most part, proud of how I'd raised this boy. Making sense of how he went from such a great kid to this horrendous point was so confusing, in an almost crippling way. The amazing person I knew was still in there. I could see him. But he was slipping away, and a whole different person was emerging.

I wondered, *How did we get here?* while feeling painfully aware that there was no one with whom I could sort out my feelings. I mean, who could even receive that kind of information? We're talking about a darkness that is so hard to describe, one that most people simply can't get comfortable with. There wasn't an "Oh, let me open up my enormous crevasse of woundedness and share it with you" option. Maybe a more honest version of that statement is, the shame and pain just didn't seem like something you "have coffee over." And maybe, in the end, the fact that I felt I didn't have anyone to chat it over with was a blessing all on its own. Because years ago, I needed the input of others in order to be clear on the decisions I made. I was frozen by the opinions of others because it was multiple people's truth. This is a characteristic of being an adult child of an alcoholic. It wasn't until I stopped listening to and consulting others on a decision I have to make, that I began to connect to my own truth and trust my own personal rudder. I have learned that the best way for me to get clear is to get clear on what it is *for me*. I use these two words regularly to both connect to my truth and express it in whole honesty. So, with this in mind, up until this point, had I confided in just about anyone that I was considering leaving, perhaps they would have been able to talk me out of it. Or perhaps I'd feel shame for it. Or perhaps or they might project the terror that would have been weighing on *their* shoulders were the tables turned.

"Maybe you should go to an Al-Anon meeting or something like that…" was the advice given by more than one person over the years. I did try that—once—and while I acknowledge that not all meetings for any particular focus are the same, I had little interest in sitting around and verbally swimming in my or anyone else's stories.

I tried to be an open-minded, willing listener. But as I listened, I kept thinking, *This is absolutely not what I want to be doing!* It just wasn't for me.

As I drove home, my thoughts pondered questions such as *How do I hold love for the addicts in my life and still own or even just stay on my path?* and *How do I still create my own story, love them and yet not step into the life they were currently creating?* (for which I had, if I may state it again, exactly zero interest). Was I required to, by their choices, alter my direction? Should I feel bad, guilty, even shameful for their choices? What did it say about me that they were making these choices? What does it say about me that I think this way?

For me, sitting in a room talking about it all, over and over, each one of us validating each other's hopelessness, felt like backwards motion. That said, talking through things, sorting things out, and hearing your own voice express your thoughts is valuable and important—for only as long as it is necessary to move you forward, should you so choose.

And that was my challenge, my quest—the fierce pursuit of my own path, of discovering everything that was still inside of me waiting to come alive, all while allowing space and boundaries and love to still be there for them...albeit differently.

"I love you, and I want to do life with you...but if this is the road you choose to go down, you will go down it without me." I didn't say that just once. And, having said it, I had to shore myself up again and again to hold to that truth, both for Andrew and for me.

I am not someone who believes that it is always necessary to dig into the past in order to heal (at this very moment, some psychologist somewhere is vehemently disagreeing with me). I believe that healing can happen as we are fiercely honest and boldly loving with ourselves. As we move forward and build toward the person we want to become and the life we want to live. As we keep moving toward the runway.

Society will want to point fingers. But at the end

of the day, regardless of "generational curses," DNA, or childhood wounds experienced, we all make choices, and we right- or left-choice ourselves into every next step we take.

At this point on this day, driving down 67th Avenue, it wasn't a matter of wondering whether I could continue to do it on my own; it was a matter of not thinking I could do it anymore, period. It wasn't a matter of taking the easy way out. I wasn't trying to end my life; I was trying to end my pain, and this seemed to be the only way to do this. Nothing was working. It was destroying me inside; there was a feeling of my heart and throat being clenched with overwhelming fear and there was no clear solution in sight. The pain lived *within* me, and there seemed to be only one way to get relief from it. [I would swear that it was raining that night but maybe that was just in my soul]

After hanging up the phone, Andrew immediately felt broken and was so incredibly worried about me. So, of course, my thoughts then turned to, *What did I just say? How could I have said that to my kid?* It was yet another one of those not-my-proudest moments, and it was also a turning point for me in terms of knowing that it was time for me to get *my* shit together. I could barely breathe. I don't remember what I was doing or where I was headed, but when I got home, he was there, and we embraced, crying, while silently knowing that neither of us had the answers.

I asked Andrew about his perspective on this experience because I know that as gigantic a maelstrom was churning in my body, one was churning in his as well, and it was important to me to listen to and really hear his experience. What's oftentimes more important than talking about merely the errors and extraordinarily poor choices someone makes is the emotional aspect of going through something and trying to wrestle one's way out of it, what it feels like to *everyone* involved. This is what he said:

This one hurts.

I had a bunch of missed calls and texts from my mom. I was off getting loaded somewhere, and she was out looking for my body.

I was in the garage at a friend's house, and I don't remember if I called her or finally answered her call, but she said, "I hope I don't make it home."

I fell to the ground and bawled my eyes out. At that moment, there weren't enough drugs on earth to get rid of that pain. Throughout my whole life, I've struggled with an acute paranoia of the worst-possible-case scenario happening. I have no idea where it comes from. If my mom didn't answer the phone or wasn't where she was supposed to be, it meant she had died in a car accident. All those fears came to my head right there in that moment. I thought she was going to kill herself, and it was my fault, and there was nothing I could do to stop it.

I remember her hanging up on me, and all my paranoid feelings creeping up. I could see her lifeless body. Every minute felt like an hour. There are no words to describe the way it felt. I wanted to claw my skin off. I wanted to beat my head into the pavement. I hated everything about myself. I kept waiting for her to call me back or arrive home.

CHAPTER 13

One evening in December 2011, I was lying in bed and my husband walked out to the living room with two pairs of shoes to shine. He always shined his shoes at night, but I thought it was odd that he had two pairs with him. The next night, he didn't come home.

I sent him a text message the following morning, mentioning that it would have been nice for him to simply tell me that he wouldn't be coming home. He said he'd gone out with the guys, and they drank too much and got a hotel room. My response to that was, "Then why did you pack a bag?" The truth wasn't hard to put together, and I knew it was planned and not circumstantial.

In all fairness, we were both doing the very best we could. He was trying to get me to talk to him about everything that was going on, but I simply couldn't. We didn't have the kind of relationship, communication, or connection necessary to allow for me to be open to him in the way he desired and honestly, I was completely numb. I'd learned to function as a single mom during the week and a wife on the weekend, and over time, this fluctuating dynamic enabled me to function beautifully in—even seamlessly between—those two separate lives. The wall built between the two lives was obvious, and I therefore learned how to function without him. That's not his fault. I remember wondering why it even mattered where he'd been that night, and this was when I got absolute closure in terms of where we were. The fact that he didn't come home and that it didn't bother me, for me, validated where our relationship was headed.

The following April, he accepted a new job out of state, and at that point I knew there was zero possibility for reconciliation. The universe took it all away from me, and to be clear, I mean that as a positive statement. When I left, there was a part of me that wondered whether maybe one day, we would reconnect in friendship and then perhaps back into love. But with this move, I didn't have to worry about it, be conflicted or burdened by it, or otherwise think about it. I had a clean slate (so to speak), and the importance of that was huge.

On a late December day, via text message, I was asked if I wanted a divorce. I replied with something along the lines of "I'm pretty sure that's not how you're supposed to approach this kind of decision, but since it's the approach you're choosing, the answer is yes." Several days later, we discussed it in a more loving way, and I am grateful for that.

On New Year's Eve I moved in with my incredible "bonus parents," Jean and Al. Jean was our neighbor when I was four years old, and at that time she was married to Burt. After my parents got divorced, and Jean and Burt got divorced, Burt began dating and ultimately married my mom. So, Jean's and Burt's children are now my stepbrother (Scott) and stepsister (Jill). Jean later married Al.

We are a classic American family.

I'd had conversations with Jean and Al about staying with them if necessary, and as New Year's Eve approached, I thought, "I'm not going to start the year in the swamp I'm swimming in right now." They were completely open to me living with them, for which I can, in part, thank my stepsister Jill. She was a bit of a conduit in getting the proverbial ball rolling. I figured that I would only live with them long enough to figure out the next step, and I felt so safe there. They both ended up being beautiful sounding boards for me as the sorting of thoughts and feelings began. I'd walk into the room and swirl my hand in the air in a circular motion while announcing, "Family meeting," and they would come sit with me and sift. An amazing and deeply connected relationship was building during this time, it exists to this day and I was and am incredibly grateful.

Breathe. I feel like I can barely breathe. Like the last fifteen months have had me in some kind of choke hold. I can't make sense of anything. I feel nothing but numb. I can't differentiate one feeling from an-

other. It's like I have no feeling. The void of nothingness that can only be found in the pitch black depths of the ocean.

Not grief.

Not anger.

Nothing.

That was my journal entry on January 1, 2012. I quickly came to realize that my normal desire to push was simply an impossibility. I had nothing left in me. It was as if I was a walking zombie (and I hate zombies, by the way. They freak me out). Even though I was far from clean-slated, I felt empty. No reserves. Nothing to draw from. Utterly spent. Deep restoration was necessary, and it was led by a fierce pursuit of pure self-love.

My sole focus at that point was simple: emotional survival. I knew that not everyone would understand my choice to leave, but I made what was, for me at that time, the only choice I could make. Because Andrew had been living with us, there was a point where I thought, "I'm leaving Andrew here with my soon-to-be ex-husband (who is not Andrew's biological father yet loves Andrew very much). I don't know how that's going to go, but I've got to take this day by day. I can't stay here with either of them right now. Something's got to happen to break this kid, and at the same time, I've got to find an oxygen mask somewhere." I simply didn't trust being around either of them, and I had to honor *everyone, including myself* by letting go a bit.

In my world, the act of honoring oneself and others has a form of practicing non-violence. What I do (and don't do) for my body, for my being, for my life comes from a place of honor and love for myself. To honor somebody else is to allow *them* to be who they are, to appreciate their essence, to let them walk their own path, to be of support, to show respect. It's a framework from which we can make strong choices. It's a priority that we either do or don't have. You might think you are honoring someone else by dishonoring yourself, but I disagree. At the end of the day, if—in order to honor someone else—I must dishonor myself, that is not honor at all. And dishonor of myself is, in my view, a form of subtle and silent violence. That may sound extreme, but think about it for a moment. Think about how it feels to honor yourself, and then think about the contrast of how it feels to *dis*honor yourself. At its very best, it's harmful.

A while back, I was invited to a local restaurant and bar with a group of people to watch a fight night. It was to be two female fighters. While I was tempted to go—to get out and to have the opportunity to get to know a few of the people who were attending—I kept thinking what a horrible experience it would be for me. Watching people physically hurting each other not only makes me sick to my stomach, I find it disturbing. This is what is true for me.

I accept and can even honor that others do not hold

the same perspective and belief in this matter. I understand there is a nature within many men (and some women) that lends itself to the conquering, physicality, and victory aspects of this activity. There is not one ounce of me that feels people are wrong for this. But for me—embracing what is true in my heart and soul—to participate in any way would be depleting to me.

I remember one day as a little girl, I could only have been eight or nine years old at the time, I had my first experience of seeing people fight. School had let out, and my mom had given me ice cream money to use after school because I had done my chores without being asked. I practically skipped to the ice cream truck, wondering if I'd choose a 50-50 bar, a Bullet. or a Dreamsicle. I could almost taste them, feel their cold deliciousness on my tongue. I could see the truck in the distance—and a crowd.

Keep in mind, as a little girl I was pretty scaredy pants. I was the four-year-old you would see holding on to her mom's leg, peeking around it as if that leg held actual powers of protection. So, just walking to the ice cream truck by myself after school was a huge accomplishment for me.

As I approached, I began to get nervous about the crowd. There were so many people, and I began to walk more slowly. I wondered if they would be nice or mean. I wondered if anyone would hurt me. I wondered why they seemed to be in a circle. I wondered why they were yelling, "Do it, do it, do it." And then I saw it: two boys, one sitting over the other with a rock in his hands, holding it over the other boy's head. The image sent shockwaves throughout my body, and I immediately turned away. I could not allow myself to see what might happen next. I threw up, and then started home, my entire body shaking. I could not believe what I had witnessed. Even writing this now, my recall is so vivid that I'm physically affected enough by the memory to feel like vomiting. This event shaped my view of fighting, and it will continue to do so for the rest of my life.

Because I have this self-awareness—because I fully accept and am honest with myself—I know that to choose to attend, even for the social aspect, would violate who I am at my core. It would honor others by dishonoring myself. And so, I declined.

Years ago, before I really understood myself and the effect different experiences have on me—whether positive or negative—I would have attended. I would have put on a face, pretended to at least be okay with it, and tried to have fun. Even knowing that every time I caught a glimpse of a fist in motion, intending to impact another human being with enough force to harm, it would take its own toll on me. I still would have gone. And, in having gone, I would have driven home fragmented, because I had made a choice of depletion.

There are things that occur in our lives every day

that violate our personal values and who we are at our core, and yet we make choices to engage in whatever that is—for the wrong reasons.

Lack of self-honor depletes. When you take the time to truly feel into what is true for you in any area of your life, to be wholly honest with yourself, you are then in a position to make choices that honor yourself. Choices that elevate, strengthen and enliven, not choices that deplete.

At many points, I've wondered whether or not part of my journey was to save Andrew from his. That's where I start to play with the idea of "soul-level travel partners" and whether we purposefully choose the souls with whom we'll navigate this journey on earth. Who knows?!

Part of my growth came from Andrew's choices, and part of his growth came from mine, which is both a silly and an interesting thought to me. With that in mind, I knew I had to be conscious of how I was responding to each instance. My past responses had been born from a franticness and a desire to control the situation. All of those approaches utterly failed in terms of helping him get on a healthy path. Things only started to change when I began to let go; when I started to just be love; when I started to accept that it was part of the journey; when I started to *be* love enough to make choices that were right for *me,* not just for him. Because making the choice that was right for me was, ironically, the choice that was also right for him, validating the concept that you can't respect another by disrespecting yourself.

I had spent nearly my entire life *not* honoring myself, instead honoring others before me, and I knew that was backwards. But in addition to there being a clear connection between being an adult child of an alcoholic (ACOA), I was also taught that honoring others before me was the one true way to happiness. I received this special wisdom from my grandmother throughout my life, and while there is truth to it, I didn't realize up until that point how backwards the principles were that I was taught by my own family, by the church community I was surrounded by, and by society.

Honoring others before yourself is not—in and of itself—wrong. But when it requires the sacrifice of who you really are and what you believe, it's absolutely wrong (in my opinion). That was the disconnect for me. I had to get to the place where I could embrace what truth is *for me.*

Shortly after moving in with Jean and Al, I began engaging in massive self-care. I knew I needed nurturing; I knew I needed to heal; I knew I needed to allow my emotions to be present; I knew I couldn't control everything. But I also knew I needed and wanted powerful distraction.

During times of reflection it became clear that I didn't realize for how long I wasn't being my fully authentic self. The stress of being detached from one's own soul can certainly contribute to an overall feeling of grave discomfort. I didn't realize how emotionally fragmented I really was, and some work had to be done in order for me to begin to own *my* truth, *my* beliefs, and *my* being as well as to truly love myself. I was willing to make the changes necessary in order to live life on my terms, based upon my beliefs, and for it to be okay for me to believe what I believed and see things the way I saw them. I suddenly realized that I didn't have to fit anybody else's mold, and that realization was incredibly liberating.

Embracing the whole of who you are is an imperative prerequisite for living a well-rounded life. I lived a fair amount of my life as only a portion of my true self. And, in an ironic twist, so did Andrew. What didn't allow me to be whole were the widely accepted but rarely questioned rules placed upon me in terms of how we're *supposed* to live. I grew up with the belief that you do this and then this and then that. I had a sense of what a good life looks like, and here was that life right in front of me, so it must be right. Right?

Andrew, however, *didn't* grow up like that. There were some fundamental differences in the ways that he and I were raised. Whereas I didn't feel like I had much of a voice and was taught how to sit like a lady and act like a lady, we probably allowed him to have *too* much of a voice and not enough structure. I didn't permit the use of the words "should" or "shame" because those words were used with me on a regular basis. Is "shame on you" not the most horrible thing to say to someone? I refused to perpetuate any of that; I wasn't going to emotionally manipulate my kid, or at least I was going to do my damnedest *not* to. I wanted to allow him to become his true self as he was growing up, and yet I was at a point where I truly didn't know how the hell to navigate any of it.

Once my second husband and I had separated, the situation with Andrew again escalated, and it was decided that he once again needed to be kicked out of the house he was occupying with him. We told him to get his shit together and find somewhere to go. At first, Husband Number Two let him return to the backyard (he was likely as much of an enabler as I was), but things weren't getting any better. Andrew's combativeness and mood swings were getting worse, so we told him he could no longer stay there. He ended up staying at a friend's house, and we went through a period of time where I was frequently picking him up to take him to the doctor because he claimed he was sick. What he was, in fact, was "dope" sick; I just didn't realize it. I floated between believing he was truly sick and knowing flat-out that he wasn't.

My February assignment for Toastmasters required that I dive into the deep end of my anxiety when it came to performing in front of a group. I had to craft a speech in its entirety, and I titled it "Embrace Your Inner Pink." At its core, it was about the truth that you can hold strength and femininity at the same time, in a powerful way. The morning of the speech, I had picked up Andrew to take him to one of his infamous doctor visits, and I was a nervous wreck about the speech. Andrew got into the car higher than a kite—and I knew he wasn't high on marijuana. I remember thinking, *Can we please just get past this?* After a few minutes, I told Andrew there was no way I was taking him to the doctor in that condition. I turned the car around and took him back to where he was staying.

As I continued on to the Toastmasters meeting, I wondered, *How in the world am I going to deliver this speech right now? I'm a mess! I know my son is high, I know it's getting worse, I don't have a clue what to do about it, and I'm on my way to deliver a speech on embracing your inner fucking pink. How is* that *going to happen?* I was still the person who freaked out if people were looking at me; I needed my sunglasses.

At that moment, a distinct thought came to me: "That's not the speech you're going to give." I can still feel the exact moment as I drove eastbound on the 101 freeway. It was one of those undeniable moments with an unintended inner dialog that absolutely felt like the spirit of God, to which I argued (yes, in my head), "*Oh, hell no.*" The thought again spoke: "That's not the speech you're going to give."

I arrived an hour early and wrote a new speech about all that had happened in 2011 and the fact that you can stand strong with feet planted, even in a sea of chaos and pain. I tossed my old speech down on the table and just went for it. Seconds in, I had no fear, even though I was sharing my inner guts with perfect strangers. It all just flowed out. Not only was it cathartic, it was empowering. As I delivered my speech, I made a mental note that the most significant part of what I was sharing was Andrew's story. I was transparent about the fact that he was living in addiction, and yet here I was delivering a speech.

After my speech, a woman named Sheila, who's become one of my closest friends, approached me and said, "You have an incredible message." We met for coffee a few weeks later, and she began coaching me right there and then. She is a life coach with the ability to guide me on how to really understand *myself* and learn a different way to exist and navigate the challenges around me. We met once a week, and I also participated in her group program. I remember a day when I was telling her about one of the assumptions I was making, and she asked, "What are you making it mean?" to which I responded, "What do you mean by 'What am I making it mean?' It means what it means!"

She was quick to clarify, "No, actually *you* give meaning to it." That revelation was pivotal.

I would focus for the entire next year on honing my inner strength while allowing myself to go through what I was going through. A willingness to step into deep vulnerability was the means through which I continued to cull and sharpen my strength. I had some tall walls up, and I had to become comfortable with the fact that vigorously pursuing my growth, which is what I was intended to do, is done by strengthening your ability to become comfortable with vulnerability. To sit in it, to be with it, to not wrestle with it, to only give it ease and breath. There has always been an undeniable warrior in me, and I've never been someone to sit around licking her wounds for long. I don't have—and have never had—any tolerance for that approach. I knew there had always been a fierce fight in me, one that could be both my best friend and my worst enemy. We each have the warrior of a lion inside of us; it's the way we choose to lead or leave that internal warrior that creates our outcome of advancement or resignation.

CHAPTER 14

1/15/2012

Pray...just pray. Just be in conversation with God. Just trust. Just slow. Just be.

Early in 2012, Andrew called and told me he was hiding behind a bush on the backside of a building. He was starving, broken, and alone. He had gotten into a fight with the friends he was staying with and had nowhere to go. As he remembers it, I had completely cut him off financially and emotionally. Every time Andrew had moved forward toward recovery, I was in, available and open to helping in whatever would also include the holding of my own new boundaries. Yet, in the moments he was clearly not moving forward, I redirected my full attention to my own path.

Coldly cutting him off as if he were no longer valuable to me felt like someone was gutting me with a dull blade. And that's the rub, isn't it? When you deeply love someone who chooses to walk this road for the multitude of reasons they do, cutting him off is...well...just not that simple.

The experience for the non-participating participant is not for the faint of heart. There are moments of frantic desperation, moments of outrage, and the kind of despair that could darken even the brightest room. You bargain, negotiate, and even throw in a few very ineffective uses of guilt under the guise of "Don't you see how this is affecting me? It's tearing me apart." Let me be clear: do not do this! All you accomplish is making the addict feel worse than he already does, which drives them away from sobriety, not toward it. It isn't about you, and you need to get clear on that right now.

For the record, martyrdom is also *no bueno*. Making your life about them—as if you have no other choice—is bullshit. You do have a choice. You have a life to live and an example to set. And while it will take every bit of your resolve, every ounce of your resilience from every cell you have, you can—and you are allowed to—live a happy life.

That doesn't mean the choices are easy; they aren't. As a matter of fact, some of the choices are downright vomitous. But they are yours to make. You set the rules for your life. You make and hold the boundaries. Speak words of life and belief into your loved ones while holding strong to your truth. Continue to walk forward and trust in the unfolding. We all need to receive this kind of powerful energy from time to time, and in giving it, we experience it as well.

CHAPTER 15

I had found Andrew a room to rent and almost as quickly as Andrew took up residence in the rented room, he had to leave it and had nowhere else to go. It was at that point when he said, “I’m done. I want to go to Teen Challenge.”

We got him admitted to the program in April 2012. It was actually right before my second husband moved, so he came to say goodbye that same day. I didn’t see or hear from him for several weeks. For the first few weeks of the program, there's no communication at all allowed between participants and the outside world. There's a complete separation, which—while awfully hard—was actually quite beneficial for everyone involved.

As his mom, I had some super scary thoughts during that time while trying to navigate both my fear and my stress, not allowing my thoughts to get too far down the path of I wonder what’s going on there right now. Yet, I felt a sense of relief because I knew that someone else had him covered. In many ways, that relief saved my life. Before he was admitted to the program, the phone would ring in the middle of the night and I’d be petrified that it was again the police, this time telling me he'd been arrested. Or was dead. Finding ways to keep myself going during that time was sometimes an hour-by-hour, minute-by-minute proposition. But, from the point at which he entered the program, I knew he had a place to sleep, that he wasn't using (thereby jeopardizing his life), and I knew he wasn't going to leave because he had nowhere to go. I could finally rest inside my own body. I could finally breathe.

I have incredible gratitude that in time he would develop whatever the "thing" is that makes one choose to take the next right step. I was also incredibly grateful that he's always had the same depth of love for me that I've had for him. I was working so hard to do what I thought in each moment was the right thing. Some days I felt like I was succeeding, and some days I knew I definitely wasn't. But I was trying all the same. To be recognized as such an anchor for him spoke to the sacred contract I believe more and more that he and I have. It's almost as though he knew, before coming here, that I and I alone could and would prevent him from making an irreversible choice in his lowest moments.

After participants have completed the first phase of the program wherein they detox and begin to become more stable overall, they leave the main campus in Phoenix to head north to a different location in New River, Arizona. It's almost like graduating to a new opportunity to continue recovering and growing.

Once Andrew had detoxed, he began to get his mind back. Addiction to drugs—certain drugs especially—causes one's brain chemistry to change. So, the belief that someone has lost their mind when they're addicted is absolutely grounded in truth. They really are a different person. Once he was fully detoxed and his brain and body began to heal, we were able to begin slowly rebuilding our relationship.

This was the period during which I learned to actively forgive. I knew that forgiveness was necessary in multiple areas—even with my father and ex-husbands—and I felt that energy of perhaps resentment, and I didn't want it in me. Knowing that I could forgive wasn't enough. I needed something more. I considered what I needed and determined that I needed a process, and the process I came up with is below. It ended up being a process I'd use time and time again over the following years.

Freely and Actively Forgive

Step 1: Take a good look at how "what happened" made you feel…

Step 2: Look at the ramifications – "What happened after what happened?"

Step 3: How did you react... lash out, go inward?

Step 4: Look at the root of why the person did what they did THROUGH LOVE'S EYES

Step 5: Ask yourself, what is keeping you from letting it go? What remains for you to learn?

Step 6: What is holding unforgiveness doing to you?

Step 7: How long do you want to feel this way?

Step 8: Explore what there is for you here. What do you want to take with you? What do you want to leave?

Step 9: Write a loving forgiveness statement about the offense and how you felt, how you want to feel, what you learned, and how you will set it free.

In hopes of helping you craft your own forgiveness exercise I'd like to share what I wrote for myself during my own healing process.

Step 1: Take a good look at how "what happened" made you feel...

What do I even focus on here? There's so much. One day, my son chose to do heroin. He made that choice. I would never have believed it, but I saw it with my own eyes. Sitting here writing this, my heart twists, my guts tighten, and tears keep coming…so many tears. My sorrow is so deep. He's my baby. I grew him in my body. How could he choose this? It's as if my heart has been pierced with a sharpened arrow the size of my chest. Part of me feels like I should hide. Part of me wants to pretend it never happened. How do I move forward toward a life I want to live...with this?

Step 2: Look at the ramifications: "What happened after what happened?"

The snowball of choice—it's never just about one person. He chose to do life-altering, brain-altering drugs, and because of that I now live with a thick fear of my son ending up in prison or of receiving a phone call no human wants to receive. Horrible images of all the horrendous things that could happen in prison or his death try to rob me of my attention as I try to put my own life back together. There is the thought of visiting my son in prison. This could actually happen. How do I make peace with that?

What most people are experiencing with their young adults doesn't come remotely close to what I am experiencing. They live in their blissfully rose-colored world. How do I find color for my life again? What does happiness even look like?

We've been stolen from and lied to, and yet this love I have for my boy makes me want to cling to him, not push him away.

Step 3: How did you react...lash out, go inward?

Inward. That's where I go, for better or for worse. It makes it hard on the people who love me.

Step 4: Look at the root of why the person did what they did THROUGH LOVE'S EYES

Deep down, he craves acceptance, connection, to be appreciated for his own uniqueness. And he, more than anything else, wants to be—to feel—loved. That is what is underneath it. That is what he couldn't put into words the day he made that choice.

Step 5: Ask yourself, what is keeping you from letting it go? What remains for you to learn?

Part of it is accepting and making peace with what I missed out on experiencing that others were able to experience, and what I *did* have to experience as a result of others' choices. That acceptance almost requires me to be okay with what happened, which is so hard to reconcile. To forgive it is to receive it as a part of my life. That is tough, and yet important and true.

I think what remains for me to learn is how to truly and freely let go. This is so hard. I am realizing that begins with acceptance.

Step 6: What is holding unforgiveness doing to you?

It's eating me up. It isn't just Andrew I need to forgive. It's also my father, Andrew's father, and myself. I feel a bit of resentment and anger, which makes me want to never get close to anyone, and I think that has thickened my wall. I'm a bit more hardened even though I feel so damn wounded. I don't know if I will be able to ever trust anyone again, and I don't even know if I want to.

Step 7: How long do you want to feel this way?

This is confusing. I don't want to feel this way. I want to feel very differently. And yet I can't see how that is possible without things changing. And, at the same time, the only thing I can change is me. And I guess the only way I can change how I feel is to change how I see it first and change the steps I take after that.

Step 8: Explore what there is for you here. What do you want to take with you? What do you want to leave?

The biggest thing is, I don't get to choose someone else's choice. Pretty simple. I take with me the realization that the choice I need to/want to focus on, is the step that would lead me closer to the happiness I seek. To the freedom I want to breathe in. My own road to happiness… It is mine to walk. I choose to love myself and to love others including my son and my father, though he is not here on this earth any longer, and my ex-husbands.

I leave the mistakes of others for them to find their

own lessons from. I leave bitterness and resentment, and I will do my best to leave non-trust.

Step 9: Write a loving forgiveness statement about the offense and how you felt, how you want to feel, what you learned, and how you will set it free.

Choices were made that caused a lot of hurt—even choices I made. At the end of it all, each and every one of us seeks for the same things: love, acceptance, appreciation, connection, to feel a sense of "I matter," and to believe we can aspire to a full life, a happy life. I want to feel hopeful, happy, passionate, fulfilled, and whole. I have learned just how important our choices are and how important it is to lose attachment to the choices of others.

I forgive Andrew; I forgive my father, my husbands, and myself. I hold love in my heart for all. I will set it free by seeing it fly freely as I step forward. Each day, I will take some kind of step toward my own wholeness. Thank you for this awareness.

When you have learned what you need to learn, it's time to make a choice. Choose both to forgive with love and to step up from the place you are in. And, when it creeps in, choose it again—let it freely fly away, untethered to you.

The first time I heard his voice after those three or so weeks during which I wasn't able to talk to him at all was the most beautiful, healing moment. I was talking to my son again—not the boy addicted to heroin, but my son. Listening to the newfound awareness he had and the things he was learning was so restorative. That conversation marked the moment when hope returned to me as it related to Andrew, specifically. It would take me a while to fully trust him again, and I was honestly glad it was a long program because I felt like he needed all those days to begin my own healing and my own personal post-mortem, so to speak, plus I needed that time to get to a place where I'd be ready when he came out.

During the program, one of the greatest things that happened to him was that he was put on a team of people that went door to door and asked for donations to the Teen Challenge program. As a result, he had to confront rejection. He learned to speak more powerfully. He had to unearth his determination in order to learn the very sales skills that he uses today. When that was happening, I thought, "This is happening for a reason." Sure enough, he met some really cool people through the experience. Of course, he met some complete assholes too, but there was one man who was so taken by Andrew after Andrew knocked on his door and he listened to his story that he actually asked for my phone number. He called and told me that his business was based in another state (Georgia, if I recall correctly), but he had a second home in Arizona, and he wanted to be able to check on Andrew from time to time if it was okay because he could see that he was a really good young man. To have all this happen and then have a stranger, who also happened to be a successful business owner, profess that your kid is worth something was really special, to put it mildly. It was like salve to a wound for me, and it was quite a confidence-building experience for Andrew. I told him that I'd love it if he would stay in contact, and I thanked him profusely.

While Andrew was in the program, we were only able to talk by phone a certain number of times per week and only during a specific window of time. It was extremely important to Andrew that I was available during those times. We were able to have in-person visits on Sundays, and I was there for nearly every one.

The first visit is deeply embossed in my memory. He had gained weight, and I was thrilled to see him bigger than he'd ever been. I remember him saying, "Mom, all we do is eat!" This was the time during which he really started to gain an appreciation for food. He'd been such a picky eater most of his life, his genuine appetite really revolved around one key (and sometimes only) ingredient: cheese. Then there's also the small but significant fact that when you're doing drugs, you never eat. I was more excited about the fact that he gained weight than anything else! It was a visible sign of progress. As a parent (most parents, anyway), you truly see your children, and to see what I'd always seen rise to this new level—not just coming back to life but recognizing that he was going somewhere good, that he was starting to evolve—was exhilarating.

I went to the Sunday church service with him, which was incredibly touching. Even though I had determined by that point that the church, as a formal establishment, wasn't for me, the religious component did speak to Andrew at the time, and that's what mattered most.

As the service began, I observed those in attendance. There was a kid sitting up front who was probably twenty or so years old, and I could feel that he was restless and almost disturbed—not mentally disturbed, per se, but something was disturbing him. I could feel what was happening inside him, and It was not good energy. I could feel the creepy movement of it. He then began to experience obvious physical and vocal unrest, and when what I can only describe as the most guttural, roaring, horrible sound began emanating from him, two men escorted him outside. It was as if evil itself was in the core of his being, and he was trying to get it out. As they did whatever they were doing outside—exorcising a demon or whatnot—the service simply continued on. I was listening and looking and thinking, *Shouldn't we be doing something about this?* Apparently not. The next time I saw that kid, on a subsequent visit, all seemed to be well. I am not condemning the program's approach at all; I'm just saying that some of those moments were freaking weird.

Andrew, however, was so steady about it; his attitude was simply one of “Mom, they're exorcising a demon.” Like, no big deal. I was thoroughly confused and honestly a bit panicked. Those were the moments when I struggled the most with the religious aspect of the program he was in. I truly believe that there's tremendous value in what the program does, and I don't care if a person’s God looks this way or that way. I don't have an attachment to needing to tell someone else what their God should look like. The method through which Teen Challenge delivers their message requires faith in Jesus. The belief is that you don't need anything besides your relationship with Jesus, and the reason you’re broken is that you need to come into relationship with Him, as He is the vehicle through which you get to God. Conceptually, that's not bad, but it also isn't the beginning and end of the answer. Otherwise, it would have worked.

Andrew was baptized while he was there by choice, which was cool because when he was baptized as a kid at church camp, he did it for us more than for himself. He continued to grow and become more confident, and the time came for him to graduate from the program. And yet, one of my worst moments, one of Andrew’s darkest, was yet to come.

CHAPTER 16

"All of us are seeking the same thing. We share the desire to fulfill the highest, truest expression of ourselves as human beings"
—Oprah Winfrey

While my inner warrior was ever-present, there was also a part of me that was completely outraged about everything. The thought that the choices made by others alongside some of my life's most profound tragedies could steal away my happiness gave me a raw and almost visceral feeling of being outright robbed. It simply seemed so incredibly wrong that my experiences should force me to take on a badge of sadness—or worse, a fractured sense of self-belief that would result in an overall feeling of unworthiness.

Each of us has a responsibility for our own happiness and for doing the work—the vigorous work—required to determine precisely what brings us that happiness. We're each responsible for our filters and interpretations. We're responsible for what we do with every experience we have, and we can either allow those experiences to move us toward the highest version of ourselves—or not.

Part of honing your strength involves vigorously pursuing your growth. It's being willing to be completely honest with yourself and others about what is *really* going on and what your part is in all of it. I recognized that if things around the house didn't get picked up for a while, anxiety would take over, self-deprecation would commence. I knew how ridiculous it was, so I thought, "I've got to make myself go through some sort of exercise to get okay with everything not being clean and straightened up all the time." That didn't mean that I had to become comfortable with mediocrity. It didn't mean that I had to become comfortable with sloppiness. It didn't mean that I had to stop striving for excellence. It meant that I no longer had to demand any or all of myself to the degree that it was detrimental to my being.

I can now look back and say with full confidence, "I know what my part was in the ending of my marriages." I don't like the word "failure" because I actually don't think of experiences in that way. But I know the events that took both of my marriages to the point where they were no longer right, and I know that I also had a role to play in those endings.

Because I'm instinctively protective of myself and those I love, I had—and sometimes still have—moments during this process wherein I put on a sort of armor as self-protection. It wanted to come down and shield me, and I had to learn not to allow it to. I had to learn how to say, “Thank you so much; I don't need you anymore.”

CHAPTER 17

Once divorced, I needed a plan to generate (and soon) an income that would take care of me. The most logical thing for me to do was go back into the insurance industry, but it just didn't speak to me. I still craved something that came *from my heart and soul,* and maintaining belief for something better (while my son was battling a heroin addiction) was critical.

I had to make a decision: continue with a small business I had been running with a friend, look for a job, or identify a third alternative. The third alternative was to decide what I was passionate about and figure out whether or not I could create a business from it. I thought through the two most logical options, which were to get a job or continue with the business we had. I wanted to do neither. I simply had an inner knowing that if I allowed myself to heal, rebuild, and get in touch with what I was most passionate about and create from there, I would be just fine. This is the belief I held and continue to hold to this day.

On November 5, 2012 Andrew, while still in Teen Challenge, attended a Toastmasters meeting with me.

He told his story and spoke about the way he went from doing drugs to talking to kids about *not* doing drugs. I had a few friends in the room, and the experience meant the world to me. After the meeting ended, I looked to the back of the room where Andrew was surrounded by attendees who were shaking his hand, offering him positive feedback. My soul was lifted.

All of that was super inspiring, but we weren't out of the woods just yet. The demon of addiction cannot simply be squashed. It has to be stared down, examined, broken apart, and stood on top of, over and over and over again.

7/1/2013

Overwhelmingly happy, he has done so well. I'm truly excited. And, at the same time, sufficiently scared. How do I help him stay on solid ground? This is the swimming of feelings and thoughts today.

Andrew graduated from Teen Challenge in June 2013, but it was only a few months before he relapsed, which I'd been warned was highly likely. When he came home, I'd put rules in place, including one whereby if he wasn't working, he would be home. When I got home one day, he was supposed to be there, but he wasn't. Everything was always fine...until it wasn't.

What I didn't know at the time was that Andrew had some money before going into Teen Challenge that one of his friends was holding for him. He had every intention of getting that money back, and he wasn't yet confident about whether or not he'd use heroin again. As I'd learn, not deciding that you're done means one and only one thing: you're not done.

He got access to the money and began hanging out with one of his old friends. When that happened, I knew we were screwed. I tried talking to him about my concerns, but he wanted to be there to "support his friends." He refused to *not* be a friend to them, and he had a really beautiful argument as to why and how that was okay. The next thing I knew, he was again getting high.

I felt frantic. My mother's intuition was fully engaged. He wasn't supposed to be driving because I knew he was using again, and I was trying to figure out how we could navigate him back into Teen Challenge or some other program. He was doing a really good job of lying at that point, and on this day, I got home from getting him something for his stomach pain, and his car was gone. I knew he was headed somewhere bad. I felt helpless, hopeless, and defeated. In fact, that was one of the most difficult moments of the journey both for him and for me.

I called him, he answered, and I asked him where he was going. In certain moments, I had a way of bringing the truth out of him. He told me he was going to pick up heroin. I begged him—and I mean *begged*—while he drove. He cried while I pleaded. I cried as he told me he couldn't do it. He didn't want to go, and yet he couldn't turn himself around. That's what that drug does to you. It compels you—not just in your mind but also in your body. You crave it so badly that almost nothing else matters. Who am I kidding—*absolutely nothing else matters* to the addict when they are using.

We stayed on the phone until he was almost there, and when we hung up, I dropped to my knees, sobbing. The counselors had told me that relapse was part of the deal, but I didn't want to believe it. I really thought that after his time in Teen Challenge he would be past it. I believed that all the time he spent in the program combined with all he went through would have been enough for him to beat it once and for all and get his life back on track. I thought that his having learned to depend on God would be all he needed.

They were right. I was wrong.

This is the second of his two lowest moments, as Andrew tells it…

I was in heavy withdrawal from heroin. My mom went to the store to get me anything she thought might help. I broke into her room and took my car keys and took my car, heading west to I-17 in Phoenix.

She called me and begged me to turn the car around. She said I didn't have to do this, that I could get through it. I started crying and every part of me wanted to turn the car around. But I physically couldn't do it. I was truly trying to turn the wheel to get off the freeway, but I couldn't. There was so much resistance from my body. Tears were pouring down my cheeks. It was as though I was truly paralyzed.

I kept saying, "I'm sorry, I'm sorry, I'm sorry" and then hung up the phone and went to get high.

I also asked for his perspective on the mindset of an addict when using:

I've heard, "Nothing else matters to the addict when they are using." To this, I say yes and no. When I was withdrawing, the moral compass was gone. When I was using, as long as I had drugs, I wasn't that much of a bad person. But when withdrawing, it didn't matter who was in the way. I'd go right through them to get to the drug. I still did bad things when I was high, but I had somewhat of a sense of morality. Or a heightened sense of it. Eventually, I crossed the threshold, and nearly all of my morality was gone.

In that moment, knowing he was driving to buy heroin, I decided to go to yoga. I still don't comprehend how I did that—I knew my son was driving around, headed to purchase drugs, preparing to be high any minute, and I had no idea what was going to happen after that. I also knew that I couldn't do anything about it. My mind had been racking itself, trying to find an answer, a solution, a bridge, anything. There was nothing. I wasn't going to dive into a bottle or even get angry, and I decided that I had to get a hold of all the thoughts and feelings I was having. I needed to open my soul in stillness so I could hear and feel God. I knew that the place for me to do that was yoga.

I realize how absurd it may sound that I went to yoga after learning that my son was on his way to desperately purchase heroin, so let me share a bit about why that decision was made and why it was so important.

Several years before any of this started, I was diagnosed with fibromyalgia among a few other things. My joints were basically destroying themselves, and it created a tremendous amount of pain. The onset of my pain was gradual, and I came to discover that my diet absolutely contributed to it. I wasn't paying much attention to what I was putting in my body from a health perspective and was consuming lots of sugar and processed foods. I didn't understand that I was essentially poisoning myself. I don't metabolize sugar well, and instead of processing it, my body was attacked by it.

I was taking a lot of medication and getting frequent blood tests, but all I could really do was lie on the floor. I hurt so much; even sitting hurt. My mind was in a complete funk. I couldn't sleep, so I took something to help with that as well as an antidepressant. I took an anti-inflammatory called Celebrex (which was eventually taken off the market), and I took medicine for pain and ended up having to take medication for GERD because acid reflux resulted from all of the medication I was taking. Finally, I was scheduled for knee replacement surgery. The day before surgery, I received a phone call alerting me that the insurance company was considering the procedure experimental and wasn't going to cover it. The surgery was cancelled.

As it turned out, the real reason the surgery was canceled was that the surgeon had a cocaine addiction. At first, I was so mad because I had put all of my hope in that solution. My thought was, "If they can replace my knee, I can start exercising again and it won't be so painful. I can also start losing the weight I needed to lose." Within a few days of the surgery being cancelled, I heard a voice come seemingly out of thin air and say, "I made the body to heal itself." The message continued to replay in my head in the same way I would receive the message "That's not the speech you're going to give" years later. I asked myself, "What do I need to know?" and immediately went to work determining what I needed to learn and do to remedy this situation on my own.

The first thing I did, which I would not recommend, was rapidly wean myself off all of my medication without my doctor's supervision. I knew things weren't going to completely turn around overnight, but I was "hearing" that it was the nutrients (or the lack thereof) causing my health problems. Understanding that our cells regenerate, I wondered, "What do I need to bring into my body to create healthy cell turnover?" I wondered what I needed to feed the cells in my body so that my immune system would become stronger and cell turnover would be powerful enough that my body would reduce the inflammation all on its own.

Next, I explored the healing exercises I could incorporate. I learned about the value of hot yoga and what happens in your body when you sweat out impurities and practice certain postures. I started doing hot yoga regularly, and let me tell you, I sucked at first. But I was gentle and forgiving enough with myself to be where I was. If I needed to lie down, that's exactly what I did. Instead of worrying about what others thought, I simply began the process of becoming present in my own body. Before I knew it, my entire body began to change. I was no longer in pain. It was likely a year and a half or two years before I felt great enough to climb mountains, but I was mentally committed and determined from the start. I committed to simply continuing until the point when I began to recognize that it was working. It became my new lifestyle.

There are two forms of exercise that have enormously helped me to heal physically and emotionally: climbing mountains and hot yoga. Through both, I feel a sense of deep connectedness, to both myself and God. I can go into a hot yoga class or step foot onto a mountain and start from a state of having no idea how I would get to the top of the mountain or the end of the class at all, but I trusted that I *needed* to be on the mat or the mountain at that point in time. In this way, the fibromyalgia, the cocaine addiction of my surgeon that prevented him from completing my surgery, the yoga that I turned to instead, all played their role. Because I would need that yoga practice for more than the physical healing from fibromyalgia. I'd need it to heal emotionally from 2011, more than I'd ever know.

As I walked into the studio, I could see the steam on the mirror. I was so fragmented, barely present with myself. This was the moment when I began to accept that this journey was *his*. And that his journey wasn't mine. An entirely new language was created around deeply accepting that one's child's journey is their own. I saw it so clearly: I cannot right choose my son into a choice I want him to make, however well intended it may be. That acceptance is, of course, so much more challenging when the child's journey includes a choice that is both life-threatening and devastating. But I had to make peace and move into the confidence that if I spiritually believed that there was purpose in all things and a higher meaning to everything and that our humanity is about our evolution and connection with God—if I truly *believed* all those things, then I must apply that knowing.

I had no idea how, in that moment, to truly accept that Andrew's journey was exactly as it was supposed to be. I also recognized that if I could accept that truth, I could move in confidence and love no matter what was happening. I knew I needed to continue to choose belief over and over, no matter what the circumstances were in any one moment.

That "knowing" was the feeling of being surrounded by the spirit of God. The blanket of Godly Love shows up for us in a multitude of ways, and this is but one of them. It was listening to what felt like words that did not come from myself. It was allowing myself to be so present, to process what just happened, and to discover what was there for me.

While practicing hot yoga recently, I found myself thinking about how yoga has been such a big part of my healing. Healing requires patient persistence. Within one's determination to heal, regardless of how long it takes, we're each given the opportunity to apply love to self. When I look back over the years, I remember my restless, impatient, demanding thoughts about why someone else couldn't make a different choice and why I should have to be as strong as I was trying to be. I remember my frustrations with how long something was taking, why it wasn't happening *right now*, instead of being at ease with the fact that it takes what it takes.

In the earlier years of my life, the way I existed in chaos wasn't working for me. Over time, I learned to have such a powerful sense of self-awareness that I can feel myself slowly seeping into that over-the-edge place. I know that if I quickly shift or address it, I'll stay in (or find myself back in) my alignment. Otherwise, the result is anyone's guess.

After much practice, this process automatically kicks in: I visualize myself with a bunch of noise around me, and I see myself getting really clear, right in the now. It's an energetic clearing out of thoughts. I then allow what wants to be addressed in that moment to present itself. I re-focus and get solid clarity on what's happening now; I engage my faith and trust. And I breathe.

These days, I can do that in a matter of seconds, but only because I've practiced it so consistently. I once had to say to myself, "Shift into faith, shift into trust," and then mentally go through the whole process step by step and far more consciously. Now, I can simply say to myself, "Shift Deborah," and the shift occurs. I'm grateful to be able to do that, because when I couldn't, the gravity of the situation could really take me down. In my life, this practice has been about getting to the point where I don't let the situations of my life weigh me down and, instead, I am able to ground down and navigate them with ease (well…mostly with ease).

I have had a connection to the intuition that lives inside of me all of my life. The intuition that lives inside of us is where our truth is. This is the center of the soul. When I went through the series of experiences throughout and on either side of 2011, I had the opportunity to practice and re-practice with wide-open arms the concept of active faith. You step and you see and you trust and then you move from there. It requires that you have courage and sometimes you have to utilize that courage in order to step and to see. You have to step before you see. You have to step from a place of "This is my truth and I have to move from that." When I do, things come into alignment.

The practice of doing that, of feeling the goodness of that, allows you to come to trust it more and more. It's not an idea that, once taken in, promptly takes life. The form, the life, comes from exercising it, from continuing to see.

When it came to my knee, the cells needed to regenerate for healing to happen, and being loving with myself through the process was actually part of that healing. When you come to that point in time in your practice where you begin to realize that you're healing and that you have strength in areas where you haven't had strength in a long time, you recognize, "I'm here! And, it took all of *that* for me to get here."

Somehow, by the end of my climb or my yoga practice, I'd have leveled out. Each practice proved the truth that simply being persistent, simply allowing the practice would help my soul heal and emotions settle. There's an anxiety that takes over me sometimes—over all of us sometimes—and these two practices allow that anxiety to settle down so that I can see more clearly. When you're in the midst of a sea of anxiety, you cannot see clearly, and it affects so many things. It affects the way your emotions show up, your radar (or perceptions), and all of your interactions, but it also affects the way that you make decisions. A state of clarity is the only *good place* from which to make big decisions.

A lot of people spend time in a yoga class with the intention of connecting, calming down, and getting clarity, but often there is a back-room head conversation that moves them to want to swiftly get out of there so they can move on to the next thing they need to deal with. I get that. I've had to practice that side of being present myself. What we need from the present moment is always there for us, but we have a tendency to leap forward into the future moment and rob ourselves of what's happening in the now. I had to become willing to play with that tendency to want to escape in order to become more connected to myself on a consistent basis. It was when I began to see the reward that came from the willingness to simply be with myself that it all clicked. In fact, the reward was two-fold. There was the reward of simply getting into the moment with myself and recognizing that there is only right now, of feeling myself getting a bit more whole and realizing that the part of me that wanted to run on to the next thing was robbing me of the feeling of being in full and true connection with myself. There was also the reward that came as the outcome of all of those amazing minutes of letting go of what was both before and ahead, simply being present. It's an ongoing practice of my humanity, and it's never-ending. It's not a practice whereby you ever say, "I got it. It's good now." I practice it every single day. It's as though I can step into anxiety or a step into the noise of what is happening in any given moment, and when I do, I become truly disconnected from myself. If I'm not observant of what's really happening, I cheat myself out of any progress I can make. I'm all over the map. I've now become so aware of all of this that I can reboot more readily.

Part of practicing presence is really knowing yourself first. And I can still stray from it, and when I do I have a feeling of being disconnected. It's the feeling of not being in the room. It's the feeling of driving down the road and saying, "How did I get here?" It's allowing too much distraction. It's allowing fear to take up too much space. Fear is going to come in, but we have to acknowledge it and allow it to be on the outside of our center ring. If we allow it to come *into* the center ring it begins to wreak havoc in our thoughts and then, all of a sudden, we're distracted by the things that fear will birth and separated from some of the things that love will birth. Love is where the true power is, so if I'm in a full state of loving myself and in full presence with myself, none of this alternative dialogue has space to ensue.

The fierce pursuit of anything requires this level of patient persistence. We often persist—but only for a whopping week, which is why consistency is so important. And why grace with self is a requirement. I recently realized while thinking about patient persistence and healing that I actually am more consistent than it might initially appear, but you have to pull back the viewfinder in order to make the scene you're looking at much wider and in order to see the whole picture. We have a tendency to say to ourselves, "If I'm not doing something every hour, every morning, every day, or every week, then I'm not consistent," but consistency isn't about that kind of rigorousness for me. For many who claim to be consistent or who are seen as consistent, it's about the rigorousness. For me, it's about measuring how many times I've done something over a longer period of time. It's about looking at a six-month period of time and seeing progress and taking and feeling a gain in momentum.

Morning routine is a big focus in a number of bestselling books. I went through this whole time period wherein I wondered, *Why can't I do that?* Like, I literally could not do it that way. And I finally had to acknowledge that I'm not wrong for that. This is where understanding one's strengths and individual "wiring" is so important. The talents of discipline and consistency are at the bottom of my StrengthsFinder™ sequence, so something like doing the same thing at 6:00am Every Single Day is a concept I have one very clear feeling about: No. We have a tendency to say, "Do it like me," or "I should do it like you," and that's not it at all. All of the approaches are good, but what's most critical is determining how we as individuals use our own talent/strength combination to accomplish what we set out to accomplish in life.

So, in the physical realm, by practicing yoga I feel myself getting stronger and being able to get into poses that I wasn't able to get into before. Emotionally, the experience has been more transformative than I ever could have imagined. I've had multiple openings, both spiritual and emotional, while practicing yoga over the last several years. I believe in the pain body and that there's a pain energy we carry until we actually allow those emotions to flow through and out of our bodies. Once they are released, we experience a spiritual opening. The emotional opening is, in my experience, the moment of actually identifying what the emotion is or what it's releasing. I might be lying on my mat, and all of a sudden, I can feel the emotion rise up from the core of my soul, wanting to come up and out. There comes a shedding of emotion, and that's all healing. It's incredibly cathartic. All of a sudden, something will be triggered, and I will likely have clarity around something soon after. That, for me, represents an emotional opening.

A spiritual opening occurs when you get into a state where there's simply nothing. You're absolutely clear, and you're fully present, and you've had a clearing of sorts and you're all that is. You can feel the presence of God. I don't get here consistently (yet), and it took me a long time to experience it for the first time. In the moment, depending upon what's happening in my world, there'll be some sort of spiritual insight, some sort of some sort of connection, perhaps a vision, just some sort of opening that allows me to see things on a higher plane. Yoga energetically levels me out. It helps my cells get into alignment, and the breath of it really helps me get centered. The physical aspect of sweating and twisting and binding is incredibly healing.

As in all things, when we're in pursuit of something, there's the effort and then there's the questioning of, "Is this really working?" And then, there's that point where we rejoice, "I'm feeling some progress." That's the physical progression. All of a sudden, I became stronger in certain places in my body, and I was able to hold postures more deeply or for a longer period of time or with more power. At this point, I really feel my body with each pose, whereas six or e*ight months prior it was all I could do* just to get through a sequence. This is where we surge. And the surge applies to every moment we have wherein we genuinely feel solidified progression. That is a feeling for which the word "amazing" simply doesn't do justice!

I've had emotional or spiritual openings related to marriage, other relationships, Andrew's journey, healing my body, and my own path. I have had emotional breakthroughs or openings about all of those things during yoga or in the bathtub or while climbing a mountain. I started hot yoga shortly after my knee surgery was canceled and I was focused on feeding myself healthy nutrients. I was, perhaps, three months into my practice. I weighed a lot more than I do now, and I was in a lot of pain. The postures seemed impossible, but I had an intuition about it. I certainly didn't *feel* progress after three months, not significant progress anyway, whereby I knew I was getting traction, but there was still a hint of intuition I felt about continuing, and simultaneously, I felt a certain amount of defeat about where I was.

At that time, I was attending twice a week. The first goal was to go once a week. Even if I had to simply lay on the floor, it didn't matter. I just had to get there once a week. Once I became consistent with that, I challenged myself to attend twice a week. I didn't worry about anything else; I only focused on getting to yoga twice a week. It took me a long time to progress to three times per week. I now go twice a week, but I also hike, do restorative and other forms of yoga, kayak and go to the gym.

In the middle of the Sumit practice (created by Sumit Banerjee), there's a sequence that's done to music. Actually, there are four sequences: one's really hard, the next one's not *as* hard, the third one's super hard—the hardest of the entire class—and then the last one's not as challenging. It's all done to music, and I remember a day when I couldn't come even remotely close to being able to do the sequences. I wondered, *How am I ever going to get where I want to be?* I didn't have the energy let alone strength. So I thought, "I'll just lay here in the heat," and I kid you not, the minute I laid down I began to quietly cry. I wasn't feeling emotional, and I'm not typically a crier. It takes a lot for that to happen. Sometimes I feel like I *should* be crying, and I wonder why I'm not! But on this day, as soon as I laid down in Savasana, there was no stopping it. I realized how defeated I was. Underneath that defeated feeling I was having while allowing myself to let the feeling flow—reminding myself that it didn't matter that I was lying on the floor while people were doing yoga all around me while I cried—I didn't realize how much I had been beating myself up for allowing my body to get to this place to begin with. There was a back conversation that was working against me, and it was so unloving. I knew that the defeat came from all of this, from this conversation that I was having with myself, and then my heart asked, "What is the loving answer to this?" The loving answer is, *In all things, love.* So, I began to change that back-of-head conversation. And back then, when joint pain was the worst challenge I was facing, I had no idea how valuable this practice would become.

What was amazing was that it felt like a magical sort of lifting, if you will. It was as though you could put the damage of the dialog in a bubble, you could put the pain and the defeatism in that bubble and watch it pop. It was still there in some ways, but it had, in essence, cleaned itself out. There was breath for me after that, and the feeling of despair and defeat never came back (as it related to my body). But I'd consciously allowed two things to happen: I allowed myself to let it come, and then I responded to what I learned. You can cry all you want, but if you don't respond to what those tears are bringing you, then all you did was have an exercise of emotion—which is not necessarily a bad thing, but being who I am I of course asked, "What's here for me?"

From that point, I began to practice having a different story. I began to shift my focus to trying to change what has already been done and not beating myself up for it. I was focused on truly loving myself for what I was doing in the moment. If I ate something green, I ate it lavishly. I thought about it and felt good about it and I practiced not allowing myself to go back in the opposite direction and instead to have full appreciation for what I was doing for myself.

My love of hiking and climbing has also greatly accelerated over the past few years. Once I healed through yoga and dietary changes from the joint and tissue damage I was suffering from, I came to love hiking and am extremely passionate about the experience of hiking. On one particular experience, I came to understand its value beyond simple exercise and time spent in nature. I came to understand that I can utilize hiking for my gain just as I could yoga. I could utilize it to help me with problem-solving and when I needed to conquer something I was struggling with or conquer a fear by visualizing it dissipating as I climb. I feel every step. I feel my quadriceps and gluteus muscles engage as well as my need to open up my lungs. I visualize whatever it is that I want to overcome, I start climbing, and I make my way to the mountaintop.

I remember one Christmas Day when I was alone. Andrew had relapsed back into addiction. I thought, "I can sit here by myself in this condo or I can challenge myself." I decided to challenge myself with an 11.2 mile hike—not to simply pop up and back down the backside of Tom's Thumb, which is in the McDowell mountains in Scottsdale, but to start at the gateway trailhead and go *all the way* to the top (and then come all the way back down). I hadn't done anything like that up until that point. Well, that's not exactly true, I did hike the Grand Canyon, down and out in one day many years ago, and I literally thought I was going to die so I never did that again. I'd done five-mile hikes, but that was it. I got myself some apples, water, nuts, my journal, and my music, and I went to have a really positive Christmas Day with myself. I neared the top, and just before reaching the "thumb" there was a flat rock off to the side. I spontaneously and intuitively decided I was going to lie on that rock. There I was, lying there, taking all of it in, when all of a sudden, I noticed a level of silence I had never before experienced. It was extraordinary—so blissfully peaceful that it might be almost disturbing to some people. It was as though every cell in my body were absorbing this incredible peace. And, in that moment, a hummingbird flew next to me. We were in the desert, and I was *way* up at the top of this mountain. There wasn't a field of flowers to attract a hummingbird. There was just this one plant with this one bloom, and this hummingbird found that bloom. Tears began to fall as I felt that this hummingbird had flown all the way up there just to find me. He found his bloom, and I found mine in my determination to climb that mountain. I don't even have any cartilage in my knees anymore, so when I really tax my body, they start to swell. I know when it's happening, and yet I was so determined that I pushed past it that day. I was deeply grateful for that experience. It was one of those poignant moments in life that's absolutely visceral. In fact, I can still feel it if I close my eyes and put myself back on that flat rock. On the hike back down, I felt so proud of myself. I felt so good. In that moment, it didn't matter what had been happening in my life. It didn't matter what was happening with my son. I had never felt more deeply connected to myself and to God. It was one of the most peaceful feelings I've had in my entire life.

12/25/2014

Sitting on this beautiful rock, where just over the edge is a steep drop down, I keep asking myself, "What is your relationship with your edge?" I can see that, to own my own happiness, to own my own life, I need to get comfortable with crossing over what I have previously viewed as the world of safety into the land of the unknown.

Experientially, someone else might have been driven on that same day to do that same hike but not stopped to allow themselves that moment. Perhaps, for them, it was about the conquest. I was so connected to myself, to nature, to the spirit of God. For me, it was about listening observantly to what I needed, in that moment, which was to lie on that rock. I could have said, "I don't have time to stop and lie down. I have more to climb, and then I have to get all the way back down." Or, I could have worried about falling off of the rock I wanted to lie down on. Instead, I *really* listened, and I was rewarded with this moving and restoring experience.

CHAPTER 18

Andrew had a girlfriend at this point whom he'd met when he was a freshman or sophomore in high school. He had joined a club swim team (that season included a ridiculous amount of daily driving—morning practice, afternoon practice, swim meets—but I honestly loved it and was blessed to be able to go to most of his practices and meets). His girlfriend was on the club team although she attended a different high school. They reconnected after he graduated from Teen Challenge. They once swam together; now they were doing heroin together, sneaking into her parents' house to sleep, staying at a friend's house, or sleeping in her car. I was living in a very small condo at the time, and one night I let them come over and, in a weak moment, told them they could stay on the floor in the living room.

I heard Andrew go outside in the middle of the night—needless to say, sleep was not happening—so I looked out my window, and there he was—in the car, right in front of my bedroom window, trying to get high with a can of air. He couldn't see me watching him. He looked so broken, so uncomfortable in his own skin, so desperate to turn off his thoughts. The feeling of sadness and helplessness that I felt was indescribable. It was a sinking of the soul that, unless you've watched a loved one destroy themselves, you can't imagine. Feeling completely alone and having no idea how to help this beautiful child of mine, I was crushed.

The next morning, sitting in my room trying to decide what to do with Andrew and his girlfriend, I heard a knock on the door. It was the police, and they wanted to talk to Andrew. They asked him to step outside. I couldn't imagine what he could have done. Massive fear smashed into my guts, and yet I remained calm, taking in each bit of information as it was presented to me.

The police came inside with Andrew, and Andrew went back to my bedroom, returning a few minutes later with a pile of clothing. Apparently, Andrew's friend had stolen an armful of clothes from a store, ran out of the store, and jumped in Andrew's car. Andrew then drove to my condo and stuffed the clothes in my closet when I wasn't there. These brilliant, under-the-influence boys didn't even consider that there would be cameras that would not only be able to see Andrew's license plate but would also be able to track me down and find his car outside of my condo.

Andrew's always had a truth-teller quality, even as a liar. It's quite a conflict. I used to call him the True Confession Kid; he couldn't stand it, but this quality saved him again and again because any time he was in a situation with the police, he behaved in such a way that he became endearing to them. They saw the truth of who he truly *is.* He was honest and upfront and told the officers what happened.

I walked outside with the police officers, and they explained the series of events that had led to that moment. Andrew was handcuffed right in front of me. I can't begin to tell you what a horrendous feeling that was. Utter and complete nausea flooded my insides. It felt as though, moment by moment, some outside force was pressing in on the center of my chest with greater and greater pressure. It felt like some invisible being was choking the breath right out of me. They told me, "He's a good kid doing stupid things. We can see it." I was grateful for their awareness. I'm afraid not all people—let alone police officers—have this level of deeper awareness of others. They told me he was very honest and respectful and didn't try to hide anything. They gave me a few minutes with him before they took him away.

I found myself swirling in thoughts of desperation, fear, and anger. All I could see was just how bad it could get from that moment. I was terrified. It felt like I was going from shocking situation to shocking situation over and over. The fact that my son was being handcuffed in front of me, in front of the condo in which I lived, you would have thought I would have been mortified. But all I could think about was him.

His fear was written all over his face.

I thought, *You've* got *to be kidding me! How are we here again? How are you still making these choic-es?* But those thoughts did not come out of my mouth. My neighbor came out and saw Andrew with his hands cuffed behind his back. As Andrew and I both held back tears, my soul feeling like it was being torn apart, he said, "I'm scared, Mom."

All I could say was, "No matter what, Andrew, I love you. You have to make it right." And then they took him away. Hopelessness was giving its best ef-fort to make its way in, but I was not going to have it. I'll never be able to describe what it took to stay steady, to stay present, to not fall apart. I had just barely begun to put my own puzzle pieces back to-gether, and his were still all over the table.

Being able to simply be fully present in that mo-ment, second by second, is what saved me from coming completely unglued. *Just be fully present right here, right now*, I told myself. *You know how to do this, ground down and get present.*

As they drove away with Andrew in the back seat, what was most interesting to me was the fact that I *didn't* fall apart, even once Andrew was out of sight. I stayed steady no matter the feelings that were going on inside of me. I noticed that my logic and emotion were one. This was the first time I realized that I had learned how to let my logic lie down upon my emo-tion, and it felt powerful. I didn't dip down into the shame of it either. This was simply a choice that had an outcome; that's how I looked at it. Don't misunderstand me; it hurt. To be clear, shame is an emotion that tried to dance with me in the moments following, but I learned that shame is neither my dance partner nor my friend. Shame brings no value to me (or to anyone) at all.

I was able to pick Andrew up that same day, which I found quite strange. You'd think that if the police knew he'd been arrested three times in a two-month period not all that long ago, they'd keep him for more than fifteen minutes. But they didn't. Also strange was the fact that he went before the judge and had to pay a fine, but because the police reported his honesty and cooperation at the time they handcuffed him and took him to the station as well as the fact that he drove the car but wasn't the one who stole the clothing (a fact documented on camera), the charge was lessened.

As we exited the jail, he was ready to use. He was wildly aware that he was continuing to severely mess up his life, and he believed himself to be a complete piece of crap. After this arrest, however, I'd utterly and completely had it. He was already on probation from the first three arrests for marijuana possession, and you'd think that this latest arrest would have violated his probation. But his probation officer had been enabling him to a degree as well by allowing his innate disposition to get the better of her, just as it had gotten the better of me. Not only had he been arrested, he'd failed a drug test. His probation officer said, "That's it. It's time for a sober home." I helped him move into the sober home and he got his old job back at a printing company. Mark, the owner, allowed him to continue to work after Andrew convinced him that he was better. He was working *and* using *and* trying to manage his life.

The call I would receive that day would be one that would shock me to my core. Andrew was battling a war inside himself, one that only he could fight and win. He left his job early one day to see his drug counselor, which was required by the court or probation officer or both. He was going to pick up a prescription for Suboxone, which is a detox drug. It was raining, and on his way there he got a flat tire that he had to change on the side of the freeway. Which, by the way, a police officer helped him with. Then, when he was just a few miles away from his destination, he passed out and drove his car into a house.

The front door of the car was just inches from the frame of the house, and no one was hurt. His car, however, was totaled. Thankfully no one was in the house at the time. Once again, there was an angel in the universe watching over my son. As soon as he realized what happened, he called his counselor, who immediately came to the accident scene; talked with the police officer; assured him that Andrew was in recovery, was sober, and was on his way to meet with him. The officer let the counselor take Andrew with him.

Andrew's boss happened to see the story on the news and recognized the car. Interestingly enough, the same channel that had interviewed us both for a story on bath salts while Andrew was in Teen Challenge was airing live coverage of my son in his crashed car. Andrew's boss said, "Please tell me this isn't you." He said he didn't understand why he kept doing this to himself, but knew he needed to go figure it out.

At that point, I had to create even stronger boundaries, and the details of this time period are a bit spotty because of that. I was still in Andrew's life, but not as deeply on any level as I had been. There were periods of time—weeks here and there—when we didn't communicate at all.

Society tends to look at an act—whether one has stolen, lied, used drugs, or simply said something in a way that was hurtful—and judge them by the act while completely bypassing the substance of the person, as if that substance no longer matters after the transgression. This is not right. This is not responding as the highest version of ourselves as human beings. Something we need to learn to do is to freely and actively forgive others. When we are in a state of resentment, judgement, or unforgiveness, we stop seeing the person and merely condemn them for the act. There have been multiple places in my life—going all the way back to being sexually assaulted—where going through some version of the forgiveness process I detailed in chapter 13 and letting that which needed to be forgiven go has been vital. After all, how can I turn the experience into my gain if I don't find a way to release most of it? This doesn't mean that I'm free of it. Our experiences are always a part of us. The difference is that, after forgiveness, those painful experiences no longer sit as a huge crevasse of pain that we're making our identity. They no longer hold the position of being the filter through which we see, and therefore, respond or react. When we revisit it, we feel it. But it doesn't, any longer, take us down.

The fact is, what we often assume about the reason behind someone's actions is partially—or completely—incorrect. Sometimes, people make choices based not on *who* they are but on *where* they are. Someone can make an appalling decision without being a horrible person. Having said that, I acknowledge that the opposite can be true as well.

The necessary adjustment by the time I was navigating my own child's addiction involved knowing what was mine to fix and what wasn't. It was making the switch between moving from fear and moving from love. It was the confirmation that came from watching things continue in a dangerous direction for Andrew when I fixed my eyes on my own road. He didn't have an awareness that I'd done that, but I did. And if I hadn't done that, if I had still been trying to frantically fix his life, we wouldn't be where we are today.

Andrew once again talked his boss into keeping the job at the printing company, and I talked his father into buying him a motorized scooter so he'd have transportation. This was, for the record, the stupidest fucking decision. A kid, who was high constantly, was given a scooter to drive from one end of town, where the sober home, to his job. He was also required to attend some AA meetings, of course. He eventually lost that job and tested "dirty," which resulted in him being kicked out of the sober home. From that point forward, Andrew and his girlfriend moved from place to place to car to place. At one point, they lived in a room and were selling shoes for someone. And at that point, I really didn't want to know what they were doing.

There was a distance between Andrew and me during this time. I was basically holding firmly to the stance "I get to have a happy life. You continue to make these choices. I love you, but I'm eyes forward, not sideways, right now."

For my entire life, I'd done what I believed I was supposed to do. I got married, had a baby, and did life in the way I was sold, which isn't necessarily bad, but so few of us take time to think about what other aspects of life we really want for ourselves. I had made decisions for or due to the influence of others. It was time for me to redefine what drove *me*, what *I* was passionate about, and what *I* wanted to experience.

Well into the process of intentional emotional healing, I began bringing myself back to the center of deeply appreciating each moment that I was in. That was part of the healing. It was the tastes, the smells, the feelings, the emotions, everything that related to being fully engaged in the experience of being human. That practice became an indispensable rudder on my get-it-together ship.

To love is being willing to let go. To honor sometimes means letting go as well. After the arrest, when Andrew's addiction was at its ugliest state, when many people would want to latch on and hold on with every fiber of their being, I knew without doubt that doing so would not have honored my son. In that moment I was honoring myself, which also honored my son, by saying, "I love you, and I want to do life with you, but if you're going to walk this road, you're going to do it without me."

Not everyone agreed with my perspective. But I had to come to fully own my truth, and that truth was "I get to have joy. I get to have my own beliefs. I get to have my thoughts. I get to draw my conclusions, regardless of what anybody else thinks I should or shouldn't do. Their judgment lives with them and in them, not within me." There's something very freeing about owning the realization that there are two perspectives you can have simultaneously. There's one that says, "Wow, I'm sorry that you're swimming in that judgment," and there's the other that quietly declares, "But it doesn't have to enter my space."

CHAPTER 19

6/15/2014

Understand, every moment is given. Every breath, every smell, everything of beauty your eyes gaze upon, every touch, glance, embrace, moment of passion. It is all given. It is precious. Life's moments are jewels. And the living of it is the treasure.

I spent the summer of 2014 in California with my auntie. Andrew was living with his girlfriend and had communicated to me that they had to move and that they both recognized that something had to change. During this period of time, I said to him more than once, "I need you to hear me. I love you, and I want to do life with you. But if you continue down this road, you're going without me." I kept having to say that, and he vividly remembers it. As a matter of fact, he told me recently that I said that a lot. It didn't feel like a lot to me, but apparently it did to him. At this point, I was no longer saying it for him, I was saying it for myself. In a way, it relieved me of the guilt of going on with my life in pursuit of what brought me joy regardless of his choices. And that is not easy.

6/28/2014

Here's the key:

When you step up, don't step back down

For the next few months, I didn't have a great amount of contact with Andrew. I had to create separation between us. I still saw him, and I still talked to him, but I was creating more space, realizing he had to choose sobriety and knowing that if he didn't, I might have to walk away. There is a deep sadness you have to contend with when you accept this truth. Telling him this was my way of getting okay with that possibility and preparing him for it as well.

One day on my walk by the ocean, I had an encounter with focus. As my bare feet touched the cool morning sand, my eyes looked ahead at well over a thousand birds in one area over the ocean. I knew there must be a large school of sardines to bring such a hungry crowd. Pelicans, seagulls, and pigeons were all competing for breakfast.

I had never witnessed such a sight in person. With each step closer, I became more and more fascinated. So much so that when I was within about fifteen feet, I slowly moved toward the water and waded out far enough to be encircled by the enormous flock. I knew that not one of them would "drop" on my head. I paused and took it all in.

Any other time, if you were to walk up to a group of birds on the shore, getting within fifteen feet of them, they would immediately flee in unison. But not that day. It didn't matter the species of fowl. They were focused; there was food for the taking and I was a mere distraction. There was no fear of me and no need to fly away. I was of no consequence, because the target was all they could see.

It's like this for the addict, in a way. When in withdrawal, all they can think about is how to stop the pain of the physical dependency, to stop the "dope sickness," the body's physical demand for the drug. That is all they can focus on until they can make that pain go away. And then the cycle of using, trying to get sober, and using again goes around and around and around.

Andrew and his girlfriend tried to get sober together at home. Andrew was so far into his addiction that his body could not handle the detox, and his girlfriend was very worried about him. I suggested she call Andrew's father because he was actually in town. Shortly afterward, Andrew was taken by ambulance to the hospital.

I wasn't able to talk with him at first, and they couldn't regulate his heart. His father texted me: "I am watching them take vitals on skin and bones." I was at my parents' house, without a car, which I unequivocally believed was God saying, "This is going down. She needs not to have a car." If I'd had a car, I would have been in the car. But I paid attention. The reason I didn't have a car was that I had planned to go to visit my parents for the weekend and decided to have the experience of taking the train to and from San Diego. As it turned out, the universe had something else in the works. Knowing he was in the hospital and being without a car to drive off in, I knew I needed to stop and think. I had a tough decision to make. I thought, Deborah, you don't have your car. Be aware of what's happening right now. Pay attention. You cannot allow your emotions to freak out. You've got to be fully aware of what's happening in this moment. As frantic as my heart felt, my mind stayed focused.

That was the first time this kind of thinking had such an urgency to it. I kept thinking, If I go, what message am I sending? What will I get in the way of in terms of allowing his father to show up for him? After all, that is one thing this boy of mine needed more than anything: true healing with his father.

Making that choice meant me not being there. Listening observantly is not just about hearing words. It's also about listening to the details of the moment that you're in. I focused on what was really happening in that moment, what opportunity there was for the best possible outcome, and whether or not I was strong enough to make the right choice. There was a real possibility that Andrew wouldn't survive. Once they got his heart regulated, he could communicate with me, but his body had started to shut down, and I had to weigh that fact into my decision.

Honor lies most in those impossible moments. Honor lies in making the harder choice. Honor at that time was in prioritizing the relationship between father and son. Honor was having reverence for the possibility that if I did this hard thing and communicated love while I was doing it, there might be a recovery. And there might not.

"But what if I don't go," I worried, "and the worst possible thing happens: he dies? Can I live with that?"

I was up the entire night praying, crying, vomiting. I questioned the existence of God, and at the same time felt such anger at what seemed to be a lack of response to my prayers over the years. I went back and forth, and back and forth again, plagued by hopelessness, despair, and a deep fear of making the wrong choice. What I went through that night can only be described as my own dark night of the soul. And in the light of day, my decision was clear. I was resolved. I told my parents that I'd made a decision and had made peace with it. Before I told them, I clarified that I wanted them to be careful about how they responded. I told them that they had to make peace with their response, whether they supported my approach or not and regardless of the outcome. I felt responsible to present it in a way that they could feel clean about their response. We were in alignment, and with that, I picked up the phone.

"Andrew, do you know that I love you?" I asked.

In a very thin voice he replied, “Yes, Mom, I do.”

“And,” I said, “I know that you love me…”

(Deep breath)

“I’m not coming.”

CHAPTER 20

10/18/14

If you refuse to work through the experiences you have, if you choose to ignore them, shove them away, you cheat yourself out of the growth that experience is intended to give you. I did that earlier in my life. I am resolved and unwilling to do that now.

In thinking about where we have been this year—all the ups and downs—I had this thought: What I gave him in silent demonstration was this: "I will stand by strong, in love, in prayer, but I will no longer support the choices that will destroy your life."

And I not only meant it, I demonstrated it with my actions. Part of that was moving forward in the owning of my own happiness, my own life.

That was, by far, the hardest decision I have ever made in my life. I had to say it to him in case he died. I had to make sure that he knew that I loved him, and that he knew that I knew that he loved me. I didn't get to do that with my sister when she died. I wasn't going to miss the moment. It went against everything one feels as a mother. I didn't allow myself to think about him lying in the bed, how my decision may have or may not have made him feel, or any other number of scenarios my mind wanted to run through. When that noise attempted to be heard, I silenced it by placing my attention elsewhere.

You'd think that experience would have woken him up. He told me he could literally feel his organs shutting down. He was so close to not surviving that you'd think he wouldn't use again.

But he did.

He was in the hospital for two days, and when he was released, his dad checked him into an Extended Stay hotel. He wasn't emotionally prepared to take him home to his house, so he got him a room while they figured out what was going to happen next. I was talking with Andrew via phone, and the very next day, a friend of his died. To date he's easily lost over a hundred friends to addiction. He didn't have a car, given that he'd crashed his into the front of a house. His father found The River Source, a rehab facility in Arizona, and they had space for him. What I had hoped would occur between him and his father began to take life. It happened slowly, but it was a beginning.

That summer I went on a lot of beach walks, did a lot of soul searching, and really felt the full breadth of the healing I had experienced. In September, I returned to Arizona. Having a renewed commitment to my personal postmortem priority, I looked back at the 2011 year and again considered what was there for me. When looking at the bankruptcy, I really wanted to take something powerful away, something from which I could advance. I decided that, first and foremost, I needed to learn how to be happy with what I had right then. I was receiving two thousand dollars a month in alimony, which was enough to pay for my rent, car, phone, and basic necessities. It left little room for any extras, but I knew that with a little outside coaching income, I would be fine. This meant that I found a way to be happy with almost nothing by comparison. I knew that I could go get a job, or I could continue to learn what I needed to learn from the experience while making do with less. During this time, I never shopped in a regular clothing store. I bought all of my clothes second-hand from a store called My Sister's Closet. That was my chosen reality for a few years. My one splurge was a new bed, because sleep is a critical part of self-care, and when you're actively practicing self-care, you don't sleep on the floor. I didn't, in fact, have to figure out how to be happy with nothing—I had people who would have helped me if I asked. It was simply my mission. I wanted to be able to achieve it.

I had absolutely no idea how things would work out, but I had to trust that it would all come together in its own time and way. At the same time, I had to trust the incredible drive and passion I had for wanting to create a business that would make a difference in the lives of others.

Andrew was still an addict, and I was still intent on building a life I wanted to fully live and love. I rented a condo and had to tell Andrew that he couldn't stay with me; that was simply no longer an option for him. I remember a conversation wherein I said to him, "I love you, but you will never live with me again." Saying that birthed the most horrible feeling and yet it also felt good because I was setting a necessary boundary for both of us. I started more formally building my consulting business while trying to accept that I might have to live life without my son because he just wasn't recovering.

So many people in my life have, at multiple points, said, "Your strength is amazing." I was recently reading an article about a friend of mine who ended up being a whistleblower on a hospital. As I was reading, I thought, "That required a truly deep strength." That's what I feel that life has brought to me: a deep strength. I believe that kind of strength is grown in all of us, if we so choose, through our experiences, and it's from that deep strength that we're able to do extraordinary things.

I spent the next couple of years healing, learning, speaking and practicing. I became obsessed with finding the tools I would use and chose to begin with the Gallup StrengthsFinder™ assessment. I began coaching people on their strengths for free. From that process, I learned that I wasn't terribly motivated by one-by-one client acquisition, and I started wondering about approaching corporations in order to coach/train/develop their personnel. I dove into determining how a business like that would look in terms of its setup as a formal business entity.

It was clear early on that of course I should work with insurance executives given the success I'd already had in that industry. I also realized that the larger part of my focus should be on the sales side of the business because that's where revenue is driven, and any approach that will positively affect revenue is one business owners are consistently interested in.

This period ended up being one of incredible strengthening. I accepted that I still deserved to be happy, and I could own that, claim it, move toward it. It was a constant exercise of moving toward my own life while letting go of any attachment to the outcome that crept in. I spent my days dancing between those two worlds—the pre-2011 Deborah and the post-2011 Deborah. I became very comfortable having a clear target and taking action, while at the same time, letting go of all expectations with regard to the when and the how.

CHAPTER 21

Needless to say, Andrew's addiction had continued. He finished his time at the rehab, moved into another sober home, and met a new girlfriend at a meeting. Right along with his addiction continued the chaos. In April of 2015, Andrew's new girlfriend learned about a rehab facility in California that they could attend together. Ironically, she was the one pushing for them to get clean. His position was that he didn't want to go; he was only doing it for her. I didn't care *who* he was doing it for, I just wanted him to get clean and *stay* clean. I was still living bill to bill trying to put together my business, and certainly wasn't able to cover his expenses to get to the rehab program.

I managed to get on a phone call with someone who was managing funds donated by a Canadian family that paid to transport people to a recovery program if they were serious about it. That opportunity was a godsend. We wouldn't be out any (more) money, and Andrew would be in this new program, out of state. Andrew's father had incredible insurance benefits through which Andrew's stay was covered. I arranged to secure the funds necessary to purchase Andrew a plane ticket to California while he and his girlfriend were living in complete chaos.

He was going to fly, while his girlfriend planned to drive. On the day that they were supposed to have been packing their stuff, when I got there to pick him up and take him to the airport, the place was an utter disaster. I knew by this point that this whole opportunity was little more than a crapshoot. There were no guarantees at all, and the likelihood that this was his time to get (and stay) sober was slim because he was admittedly only going for her.

They were barely packed, and there were boxes and clothes and dishes strewn everywhere. Instead of taking him to the airport, I had to get all of his stuff together. I started cleaning the kitchen, which was piled high with dirty dishes, and then grabbed some boxes and started filling them with his stuff while asking what was his and what was hers. They had to be cleared out of that apartment that day. I called his father and told him I was taking Andrew to the airport, and he was going to have to come to the apartment and pick up all of Andrew's extra stuff. He couldn't, so I had to pack it all in my car and take Andrew with me. As we got in the car and drove away, his girlfriend was watching out the upstairs window. They had both been teary while saying goodbye, but I have to be honest, I had no sympathy for either of them in that moment. I just wanted him on the plane.

This was the second time I'd put him on a plane by himself and felt physical agony until I knew someone on the other end had picked him up. He was just a little kid the first time. He must have been ten, and I sent him to California to see my mom. It was the most agonizing experience of my life, at least up until that point. I literally laid on the floor in my house feeling such suffering because he was on a plane all by himself. The moment my mom said, "We've got him!" I finally exhaled.

After saying goodbye, I stood at the airport watching him go through security, although he didn't know I was still there watching him. I could tell that he was completely messed up, and knowing that a person heavily influenced by drugs or alcohol does stupid things, I thought, "Please don't say something stupid." He was stick-thin, wearing jeans with a shoelace as his belt, which he thought was super cool. He had on a long-sleeve plaid shirt, and he kept fidgeting with himself, trying to act tough. All I could do was pray and let it go.

As I drove away from the airport, just as it happened when I was driving to my first big Toastmasters speech, words clearly entered my head. "Deborah, you have to model the rise." I had begun the process of becoming a certified StrengthsFinder™ coach, and I knew what I wanted to do; I just had no idea how to get there. I felt clueless, but I knew that Andrew needed to see it—my rise. My triumph was as much for him as it was for me. Because in that moment, there we both were, starting from nothing. He was ultimately in it for his growth, and I was in it for mine.

The process of practicing active faith most came to life during this time when I was choosing my next career—an impactful one that would help others—while Andrew was in California in rehab. I was accepting that Andrew had his own journey, and I had mine. That was when my faith caught life and I could see it. The subtlety of motion that comes from continuing to move forward in belief and seeing the result of that was enough to keep me going. It's one thing to believe you can hike this kind of mountain and go do it. It's a whole other thing when you have a son who could end up in jail or dead, you have no money, and you are still choosing to believe that you can build something from virtually nothing.

CHAPTER 22

As I was honing my understanding of the niche market I would serve, I knew I needed to work on reconnecting with key relationships, because relationships are where all things begin. I sent a LinkedIn message to someone who lived in San Diego and had worked for me when I was at Minico, asking if he'd like to get together for lunch the next time I was in town. I hadn't connected with him much since I left that job. In fact, the last time I'd seen him was when I ran into him a few years earlier in front of a movie theater of all places. This is one of the reasons I so deeply believe in trusting the unfolding of your story and that the dots will connect when they need to connect.

A month later, he and I met for lunch, and I listened as he talked about what was going on in his world. Before I attempt to sell anyone anything, I want to know what's important to them, what might be needed and in what way I might be able to help. I want to know if I am a fit for them, and if they are a fit for me. After lunch, I told him that I loved seeing him again and looked forward to keeping in touch. As I thought about it later that day, I realized that I could come in and help him with some of the things he was struggling with. I sent him an email to that effect, laying out how I could help and the way I thought the relationship could look. We had multiple conversations after that, and I put together a formal proposal for the partners with recommendations and testimonials.

He ended up saying, “I want to work with you, but probably not until after the first of the year.” I didn’t get a signed contract until December. But I did get that contract, (and they’re still clients of mine today; they are amazing people to work with).

Andrew had been in rehab for five months, and I was at the point where I had no idea how I was going to pay my rent. While I was figuring out what this whole “model the rise” concept even looked like, I knew that this was where the rubber would meet the road. I didn't know how it was going to unfold. I knew that there was a good possibility that I would get the contract with Teague, and I needed to continue to believe, but I was still scared shitless that I wasn't going to be able to make it all work.

I knew that I was at the point where I absolutely *had* to get a corporate client or I was going to become homeless. At one point that summer, I even found myself at the food bank in Carefree, Arizona, wondering how I was going to pay my bills in September and October. My alimony had been reduced, and I was not in a place of confidence to pursue the type of clients I knew I wanted to go after. I didn't know how I was going to cover rent, and I was further terrified because I had no credit. I was mortified at the thought of going to my parents and admitting that I couldn't pay the rent. When it came to asking for money, the only thing I felt okay about asking for help with was my certification, education, and business, which I both intended to and did pay back.

I reached out to two friends and said to each of them, "Here's my scenario. Let's figure something out. Get creative with me." I wasn't approaching either of them for money. My girlfriend Brett sent me an amazing message saying, "You have everything you need to go make some real money right now. Go do it." It was that sort of kick-in-the-ass motivational I-believe-in-you call to action.

My friend Shawn asked, "First of all, how much is your rent?" Not only would I not have asked for the money, I didn't even think of it, and certainly didn't hint at it. What I was looking for was an idea, a plan, but he insisted on paying my rent. The memory of that lifeline can still moves me.

That generosity did more than pay my rent. It brought me the feeling of not being alone, of knowing another person in the field of divine resources was there for me. It gave me the energy I needed, the breath of love in a moment where fear was making every effort to stake a foothold. Instead of fear, I felt the blanket of God's love, and that blanket shows up for us again and again and again; we only need to be willing to see it. Fear would have compelled me to back down, change direction, cave in, go get a job. But that was not the direction in which I was going to head. This lifeline appeared at the pre-flight moment, and having this new fuel onboard was precisely what I needed to be able to let go and catch air.

We were both on our respective paths, taking flight. We were on the runway, in motion, but not yet off the ground, and certainly not yet peacefully coasting at that flight's target elevation. While you're catching speed and then climbing, there's still a good amount of uncertainty. There are birds that can fly right into the dang propeller. I had a deep crevasse of fear to leap over in order to go out and get more client contracts. I had to grab the courage necessary to do so, and there is no motivation greater than needing to set an example for your own child.

As with most recovery programs, there is a period of time where you cannot communicate with them at all. It might have been thirty days in this case. In our first conversation, I could tell he was getting his mind back. He told me a bit about what was going on, and I told him that I didn't know when I could come out, but I would as soon as I could.

"Andrew," I said softly.

"I know, Mom."

"Last time," I said.

"I know," he responded. "I'll do it."

The second I said his name, he knew what I was going to say. He knew this was it. He knew he had to get it done this time.

His first test came when his girlfriend, through a certain choice, who was in a sister program in the same general area, had significantly broken trust with Andrew. He found out about this through someone else. I thought, "Here we go, this is a make-it-or-break-it experience right here." It was certainly enough to drive him back into addiction—for an addict, it's an agonizing yet effortless shift in direction. It's the go-to pain numbing salve.

As it turned out, *she* relapsed; he didn't. Surprisingly, he said that he instead started evaluating his life and recognized that if he was going to get somewhere, he had to make it happen for himself, not for someone else. He dove into the program and really started working it, consciously going through all the steps.

The beginning of any flight is challenging. The beginning of Andrew's biggest flight to date was getting on the plane to go to rehab. He was going to get what he would need in order to make his journey less turbulent. For me, it was driving away and hearing "Model the Rise" and not fully understanding what that meant or what it was going to look like. I was still in a place, in that moment where there was so much uncertainty in my own life. I had built the foundation of my business to a point but hadn't yet fully stepped in. I had planted the seeds necessary to ask for a big contract, but I didn't yet have it. My income was at its riskiest point ever.

There's a runway to the rise. You don't just take flight. The key is to get in motion and let the pieces unfold and move as they are designed to move. If you get into motion and pay attention to what happens, moment by moment, your choices begin to create momentum. You can make the necessary shifts by being steadfastly present. One of the most powerful skills in the world to be able to apply is to have a multitude of things going on and yet be able to get present with what's in *this* moment, right now. I could divert all my energy, effort, emotion, and thoughts toward things I can't do anything about in the right now, but because whatever is truly *my* present moment, I'm there with it. Navigating life with that framework feels so much better, and it's so much more effective. It's what allows you to continue on and say, "I can't believe how much I accomplished—even while all that was going on." We do what we subconsciously know to do, until we consciously choose to do otherwise.

I put everything in storage and my friend Deanna allowed me to live with her for a short time in Scottsdale before I headed to Lisa's in San Diego. Allowing myself to just breathe in that space during that fall was part of the ascent. The incredible thing about my friendship with Deanna is the fact that both of our sons were in the fight of their lives with this disease. We felt bonded to each other, walking the road toward our own happiness while doing what we could to encourage our sons' rise out of the swamp. This period of time is interesting to me. It was by far the worst position I had been in financially, and yet it is a period I am very fond of. She and I spent many nights on her two couches, sharing, laughing, and crying. The bond we have built will last a lifetime.

I shared with her the "setting free meditation" I wrote, and now I'd like to share it with you.

A Setting Free Meditation for Parents

It's simple, really. You go to a place of quiet surroundings, maybe out into nature, but you can do it on your couch too.

Sit comfortably, quiet your soul. Then, visualize your child in your favorite time so far. Connect to the loving appreciation you had then.

Now, from your soul, speak these words...

I love you.

I've given you everything I have found to help you on your journey.

You have what you need now, and you will find and uncover what you will need later to navigate this life.

You don't need me. Now you need you and divine

guidance.

I trust God's guidance for you and with you.

God and my universe of angels, I release him back to you, for he was never mine.

Thank you for letting me be his mother/father. I trust that no matter what, his journey will unfold for his highest good.

My son/daughter, I set you free. Go live your life, unfold your journey, grow boldly, love fiercely, and live courageously!

I am always here, and I set you free.

***

Repeat it several times. In your mind, see your son/daughter flying free like an eagle.

Let yourself feel what you feel.

Let it rise up and out.

Bring love in.

Bring trust in.

Bring gratitude in.

Now...own these words.

I am a strong woman/man with a beautiful soul, and I was and am a beautifully loving mother/father. I planted seeds, I made mistakes, as all parents do.

All is well.

Allowing for and building a healthy tribe happened over time. It was genuine, natural, and I would not be here today without the support and love of some very special people. When you open to the alignment of souls, the tribe available to you is beautiful. To make time and space for it and to honor yourself in the building of it is all you need to do. And when I say this, "Honor yourself in the building of it," I am referring to the practice of seeing others with intention. That can be accomplished through a small amount of inner research. Who is the person in your life? How safe do you feel with him or her? Who do you need to invest in? Who do you need to create loving space with? Who do you love having in your world, and who is merely an acquaintance? Who do you love, and yet not quite trust? Allowing people to be exactly who they are, not judging them as a being but instead honoring yourself in the truth of how healthy it feels for them to be in your proximity, is so important in the building of a healthy tribe. It doesn't mean that you push out of your life everyone you don't want in the center ring with you. It means you have full awareness of the landscape in the field around you. Again, the blanket of God's love shows up in the variety of ways people show up for us. We are the field of God's resources.

Andrew was growing through the process of building his own healthy tribe. He was also learning how to allow feelings to be present while "situations" occurred in his life and learning how to slow himself enough to confront each situation and then choose the next right step. He continued making better choices every time there was an opportunity to do so. He found a way to continue to rise. Our relationship changed significantly. I learned just how much he didn't want me to parent him but instead to listen deeply, encourage him, support him, and offer good questions. I marveled at his growth. He found a reason to keep pushing toward each flight's cruising altitude instead of letting go of the controls and letting life (and gravity) take over until the inevitable crash.

CHAPTER 23

1/2/16

I am alive.

I love who I am. And I love all that I am. I have earned all that I am, because I fought to become who I am. I am proud of all that I have overcome, and grateful for all the mistakes and humanness that always shape me. I am taking my life beyond the boundaries I have been living in. All boundaries: physical, mental, emotional, spiritual, experiential. Status quo living is not for me. I do not follow the crowd or take on another's beliefs because of their conviction. I must feel that conviction within my own being. I push boundaries, and challenge my perceptions, beliefs, and abilities. What is within me that does not serve me, I will wrestle out. I am focused, driven, and inspired. I am creating my life based upon my vision, desires, and dreams, on my terms.

I know with zero doubt that God watches over me, and it is under that protection that I feel fully free to be me.

I Am Alive.

One must know in the core of their being that their

story—the chronological story of the events of one's life—is not their life. One's life is the essence that he or she takes from those stories and what is done with that essence. You can choose to attach whatever meaning you want to individual events, so you must choose wisely. Often, parents or loved ones going through the battle of addiction wear a cloak of shame, believing that they don't deserve to have a happy life. That belief is utter and complete bullshit. I believed that way too for a period of time. Until I didn't.

One day I simply paused and asked, "What in God's name just happened?" and then declared, "Let's breathe now." I concluded that being a prisoner to this chaos was unacceptable, and that was a stake-in-the-sand Oh hell no moment. Just because a person in my family chose a path, I didn't have to go into a state of depression as a result of their choices. I'm not saying it's easy (or even possible) to live in a state of bliss when the person you love most in the world is struggling with something this fragile. That's not my point. My point is that not pursuing the things that bring you happiness and not enjoying the moments you're in is so dishonoring to yourself, and in my view of life, that's not how it's intended to be. We each get a path, and we each decide what turns we take. The lessons are there for us, and we each get to decide what we're going to do with them.

Andrew got to decide, "Am I going to heal or not?" Others got to choose for themselves as well.

And I got to choose for myself. I got to have a life. I didn't have to give up everything simply because of other people's choices. The first piece of the flight is coming to truly understand and embrace the truth of the individual's journey. If I truly believe that I am a spiritual being having a human experience, I must also recognize that my human experience is here for me—even though part of it is my collaboration with other people. Therefore, I have universal permission to govern the body of my experience, as does every other person. If I trust that truth, I must also trust that, for whatever reason, this was part of Andrew's journey. This is his path, and I got to decide how far I wanted to walk alongside him on that path. That's what I got to choose. I couldn't (and can't) "right choice" him into any kind of behavior. He had to choose it for himself, just as my dad had to choose for himself, just as his dad had to choose for himself.

The more successes Andrew had and the more he got up and shared at meetings, being authentic about his experiences, the more things started to positively unfold for him. That became a new kind of routine for him—a healthy one.

He got a part-time job at a restaurant as a host, and I recognized that he was truly starting to live his life separate from the environment that he was in and separate from me as well. Because he was on his own like that, I recognized that, once again, whether or not he'd stay sober was a crapshoot. But I also recognized what was possible if he kept fighting in order to figure it all out. My hope was that the more he got a taste of sobriety and the idea that life could be good in sobriety, by some miracle the more he would want to stay on that path. He's had moments, of course, but everyone has moments. He's figured out how to navigate them.

The first time I saw him was mid-summer. It was my birthday, and he knows I love kayaking. We've had some great kayaking adventures over the years. When he came out of Teen Challenge, what I wanted to do for Mother's Day was kayak Tempe Town Lake. We did that, and it was amazing. So for my birthday, he planned for us to kayak in Newport Bay. First, he took me to the restaurant where he worked and introduced me to everyone. He was so proud, and it was truly an amazing feeling. We've always had a relationship wherein we'll goof off, trying on funky hats or glasses, so we went to Fashion Island in Newport Beach, goofed around and laughed, generally so happy to be together. We then went to lunch, then kayaking. It was an amazing day, and I felt like something was finally different. I knew things were different than they'd been when he came out of Teen Challenge. I felt an essence of "I'm starting to take charge of my life" growing in him. He wasn't quite there yet, but I could feel this difference, and it was so incredibly encouraging and exciting.

Andrew's strongest inborn assets are, first and foremost, his ability to connect with any human being on the face of the earth. Second, he has a relentless willingness to be authentic—even if that authenticity is not within what is deemed as acceptable (conformist) behavior. His ability to entertain people—to be spontaneous and incredibly funny—has allowed him to bring levity to some extremely dark moments. At his core, he has a drive and a desire to make a great life for himself and others. Add to that a deep wisdom and ability to put thoughts and ideas together rapidly. I knew that once he got on the right track or in the right groove, if only he could find what that was, he'd find his way.

When he was younger, he felt such a strong desire to fit in. As he got older, he learned to embrace the things that made him different and be authentic instead of self-conscious about them. He still goes through some of that struggle; he's still aware of feeling different, but he was able to adopt the tools necessary to navigate that. He learned to embrace his unique qualities.

When it comes to women, his ability to open his heart and share his feelings in a relationship is a huge asset. When he was younger, that sensitivity wasn't a dynamic that girls were looking for, and I knew that some painful moments would come in teaching him how to manage those feelings. Ultimately, as a grown-up, this quality makes for better relationships.

He began figuring out who he authentically is, and he will of course continue to figure that out—as we all do—for the rest of his life. Once he became truly willing to figure it all out, it started to click, but it required a willingness to navigate some hard steps and then confront himself with the choices he made. He had to learn to embrace the aspects of himself that are amazing. He's wicked smart, and his mind moves incredibly quickly. He has so many beautiful, amazing qualities, and yet he undermined himself for years because his point of focus was those things that made him the most vulnerable.

The time came for him to move from detox into a sober home. He was still part of the program, but his insurance would only take him so far in the program facility. Ninety days really isn't enough time for a sustainable recovery especially with no clear plan (as we'd learned), so he started figuring out what he could do to earn the money necessary to stay in the program. I couldn't help him financially at all at that point, so he had to figure out a solution.

His father was willing to help a little bit with Andrew's costs, but his tolerance was much thinner even than mine by that point. There also came a point when Andrew no longer wanted to ask his father for money. The biggest moment of respect he'd ever experienced with his father was when he no longer had to ask him for anything, when he could stand on his own as a man. Getting to that point (and staying there) became incredibly important to him. It was okay for him to need me as his mom to some degree, but he had a deep desire to have that acceptance and respect from his father, and to this day, he still has it. So even if he has moments now wherein he's not completely sure if the month will pan out as expected financially, he won't ask us for help. He works it through and figures it out.

In hindsight, my inability to assist financially and his father's resistance to doing so couldn't have been any better of a reality because it put us both on the right track in terms of the ability to determine where, as a parent, you need to help and where you should not help. You have to learn to know the difference and that's the art, the delicacy, of parenting through addiction. It's understanding how not to be an enabler and instead how to be love. To know when someone truly needs support and when they've got to figure something out on their own. It was a dance I was getting better at.

I was beginning to figure out the puzzle pieces that I was going to purposefully put together for myself. Just as Andrew was getting traction in his sobriety, I was getting traction in my business and life overall. We literally rose together. To me, that's the coolest part of the entire experience; we were in step with one another, though not intentionally. There have been moments when I've said, "Andrew, you have no idea how much your successes are feeding me right now."

Each time he took a step, even if he had a step back, I was there saying, “You’ve got this, keep going,” and vice versa.

CHAPTER 24

I've known my friend Lisa since Andrew was two. She's been with me through all of my trials over the years, and I've been with her through all of hers. She lives in San Diego, and as it turned out, she'd had an intuition that I would soon be coming in her direction. I hadn't ever said that I was coming, but she began to prepare her spare room because she somehow knew that I was going to be coming to live with her for a bit. She told me I could stay as long as I wanted, and that at some point, when I felt like I was in a better financial place, I could start paying rent for the room. Was I ever blessed with the right people at the right time, from my bonus parents to my besties, opening their homes to me when I needed it most.

I went to San Diego that December and started my contract with Teague Insurance in January of 2016. By April, I was able to start paying Lisa rent, and my life continued to re-build from there. Little did I know, one of the most glorious gifts of my life was about to show up.

After I'd been living in California for a while, business was good, and I thought, "I'm going to create a Match.com profile, because why the hell not?" I was *very* into my profile creation—what pictures I was going to use, what I was going to write about myself, overall how I was going to present myself because, by this point, I was in the practice of *owning* myself. I spent too many years not fully knowing, let alone owning, who I was (and am) inside. This exercise brought me so much closer to meaningful awareness of myself. It was as much an exercise of bringing refinement and clarity to the expression of me as anything else. I didn't care *what* people thought. My position was, "Let me tell you who I am. You either like it or you don't. I don't care either way."

One guy sent me a note that said something along the lines of "You sound kind of high-maintenance, but I'll take you out for dinner." I thought that was hysterical. No thanks. I wordsmithed my profile almost to death, but I barely paid attention to any messages I received because anytime I was notified that I'd received one, I'd look at the message and quickly think, "I don't have time for what that message really means—that I'm actually going to have to meet somebody." One Thursday night, I was lying in bed, and I thought, "I'm just going to go and look at people's profiles." What can I say; I was bored.

I started scrolling, and a picture of a man whose profile name was *Lost Cowboy* popped up. You know how you look at a series of pictures, and the first one is great, but then the next couple start to go downhill?

That didn't happen. A few pictures in was one of him wearing scrubs, and you could see that he has shoulders like nobody's business. I have a thing for arms and shoulders as well as a bald head. There is a subtle reminder of the feeling my grandfather, Ray Gerard, gave me as a child. He passed away when I was six, but I remember the warm, accepting, loving look in his eyes when he saw me. It was an amazing feeling. I also remember the day I was told he had passed. My mom came to get me from a friend's house down the street and told me while carrying me home. I remember feeling so sad and yet so comforted at the same time.

Back to Lost Cowboy. With those visual assets, I might want to make someone naked if those areas look good, and they looked *really* good. So, I did something I'd never done. On his picture, I commented, "Man, that is one handsome face" because it's exactly what I thought. Within seconds, he wrote back, "Nothing like your incredible pictures!" Game. On.

It's important to note that, just a few years earlier, I would have been in no position to confidently engage with this man. I have a funny and fond memory of a very special friend of mine named Marie. We met at Lifetime Fitness, a gym in Scottsdale, and one night decided to go to happy hour. Keep in mind, I was married, then single for five years, and dated only minimally during that time. Then I was again married, again divorced, and hadn't yet started dating. There we were at happy hour getting to know each other, when she suggested we talk to some guys a few tables over. I immediately asked, partially petrified, "You mean you want to go *talk* to them?", as if she had suggested I eat a poisoned apple. She chuckled, said yes, and we did. And guess what? I didn't die.

From that moment, we began to banter. He had just moved to Bakersfield, California for a contract (he's a leader in the healthcare space), which was four hours away. I said something along the lines of "I think I'm in a state of depression because you've just moved to Bakersfield." Twenty-four hours later I received a text from him (by that point, we had exchanged phone numbers; I've saved his side of the entire thread).

What are you doing?

I let him know I'd just finished a hot yoga class and was having dinner with my friend Lisa. He said that he had driven down from Bakersfield and was hoping we could meet for a few hours. While this admittedly freaked me out a bit, I also had a comfortable "knowing" about him. There was something about our interaction that I knew was different. I texted back:

> *Here's the deal: I'm at dinner, and I took hot yoga so I won't be ready to meet you until 8:00.*"

It was only 6:00, so he was going to have to wait for two hours. I figured if he was willing to wait for two hours, I was happy to meet him for a beer. I went home and did my hair because it looked horrendous. I remember every detail of that first meeting. I wore my hot jeans that made my ass look really good and a flirty blouse. Keep in mind that for a couple of years before I met him, I'd been working on a sort of document that described Deborah's exceptional man and Deborah's extraordinary relationship. It was a working document that I continued to modify as I learned more clearly what I did and did not want. By that point, I had an extremely clear understanding of the kind of man and the kind of relationship I was looking for.

There was something electrifying about the banter between us from the beginning. I knew it was different, so I was excited to meet him in person. There was no doubt in my mind from the way he was engaging with me over text that his interest level was the same as mine.

When I walked up to Stone Brewing Company in Escondido, he was standing outside waiting for me. As soon as I saw him, my first thought was, "What a gentleman, standing outside waiting to walk in with me." God, I love the qualities of a true gentleman. We said hello and hugged, and I felt such a warm energy in his grip. I was immediately so comfortable, and as we walked inside, he gently guided me by putting his hand on the small of my back, inviting me to walk in front of him. We got to our table, and not only did he have the look I'm attracted to, he also listened to me in a way that was so fully present. We were so engaged in getting to know bits and pieces of each other. It was the fastest four hours I could remember. We shared appetizers, but I didn't even care about them. I remember that the Brussels sprouts weren't very good. Before we knew it, they were stacking chairs and the place was empty.

He walked me to my car, and we engaged in the typical "I really enjoyed talking with you tonight" conversation, and then he leaned in to kiss me with an energy that was so steady and intentional. We kissed in exactly the same way, and it was the most delicious, magical kiss I've ever had in my life. He backed up and said, both excited and curious, "We're in trouble." We had great conversation, but we also had a unique chemistry that still exists today.

As I was driving away that night, he texted me.

That couldn't have been more perfect.

I responded that I felt the exact same way. We have an incredible relationship, an incredible communication style, an incredible partnership. This man's touch is still like restoration to my soul.

A month or so in, we went on an amazing date at a delicious sushi restaurant. We stayed in a hotel because the restaurant was in Newport Beach, which was the midpoint between us. His son lives nearby in

Laguna Beach, which is near where Andrew's program was based, so it was convenient for a number of reasons. I was going to see Andrew for Mother's Day, and this was our first "real" date after meeting at Stone Brewery.

Staying in a hotel with him that early on was a big deal for me. I was not going to sleep with him even though we had an undeniable chemistry, and I had a conversation with him about that. He's always had an ability to sense a change in my energy, and after we checked in to the hotel, he said, "I can see that you're struggling. Tell me what would feel good to you in terms of how long we wait?" First of all, who asks that? Like, who are you? I said two or three months. We settled on three; it ended up being two. He was so genuine about what was best for me. The way he consistently, intently listened, the way he considered me, it was all so incredibly endearing.

While Bradley and I were an incredible match from the start, we did have some hurdles to overcome. I had trust issues given the series of experiences life had brought over the years. When you meet somebody online, it's a bit of a double-edged sword—especially if you like them. There's still the possibility that they'll continue to interact with others online, even continue to date others, which I suppose shouldn't have bothered me, but to be honest, it did. With the "active" feature on Match.com, I could see if somebody I was talking to/dating was still actively online (as in, at any given moment), and it became a point of conversation between us. Even though we'd only known each other for a short time, we were in communication with one another every single day. I was determined to do this relationship differently than those before it, and that meant that I was going to express my experience in the sense of "Here's what does or doesn't feel good *for me*."

I learned to express things from that standpoint, which has been quite significant in our relationship. When I saw that he was still online, I wanted to have a conversation about it because I wanted us to be authentic and upfront. For most guys, if—at the sixty-day mark—you're already wanting to have a conversation about whether or not they're online, they're hitting the road. But I was committed to being true to myself, whether he liked it or not. It wasn't about what he should or shouldn't be doing. It wasn't about condemnation. It was simply me telling him that I saw it, it made me super uncomfortable, and I wasn't sure what to do with that feeling. I described it by saying it made me feel a bit wobbly. That allowed him to comfortably step into the conversation because there was no blame or fault being placed. It was just me expressing the experience I was having, *for me*.

He never got reactive or defensive. He never shut me down or made me wrong. He has this gorgeous, steady quality about him. Instead, he expressed his side and his experience, and I could see where his experience was versus mine and where there could be a bridge of understanding built between the two. I found this first discussion of differences fascinating, because it was so very different from any communication I'd experienced in past relationships. We've always been able to navigate to and from that place, and for me that has been so incredibly powerful. In the end, it was one of many reasons I fell in love with him.

Once we'd had the same conversation two or three times about him being on the dating site, I was finished having that conversation. He'd told me that he wasn't spending time online, and yet that wasn't what I was seeing. I wasn't trying to be ridiculous about it, but at the same time I wanted to know that I was interacting with somebody who was being honest and authentic with me. If he was going to date other people, I simply wanted him to tell me that so that I could decide what I would or wouldn't do based on that information. Just be upfront. That was all I was asking.

Six or so weeks after the trip to Newport Beach, we had another conversation about the fact that he was still online. That felt like a conflict to me, and I decided it was time for us to end. I simply wasn't willing to continue on like that. It didn't feel good. To me. The whole internal dialogue that was going on combined with the emotions that were spinning out of control because my logic wasn't present was ridiculous. We had a date planned, but because this wasn't the first time this had happened, I was finished with it. He told me that he wasn't going to stay on the dating site, that he didn't want to date other people, yet there he was, still on there. It represented mixed signals, and part of my new approach involved *not* doing mixed signals. I got to decide for myself whether or not a relationship felt good. So I cancelled our date.

He was coming down from Bakersfield for some scuba certification stuff (a dive master at the time), and my message was, "Get a hotel; you can't stay with me." While it might sound like I was cold, I was in absolute agony over the situation. I was stoic and bulleted in my expression, saying, "I can see that you're on Match again, and this just isn't something I'm into." He was confused and disappointed, and at around 4:00 the next morning, I sent him a text message because I couldn't sleep. I said something to the effect of, "My heart's hurting, I can't sleep." He immediately replied (he was awake as well) and said, "We should talk," so we agreed to meet at a park area down by Mission Bay where he was going to be doing the scuba stuff.

We sat on a blanket, and I shared my experiences that had led up to that point while he shared his. For him, being online was kind of the last thing to go because, not knowing where we were going, he didn't want to cut off all possibilities. There was such a deep honesty to what he was saying and the way he was saying it. I said that I didn't know what I wanted to do, and he agreed. I suggested that we could convert to being friends because I'd certainly done that before, and I really did want to have him in my life. He agreed that we *could* do that, but that wasn't what he wanted. At that point, we both declared ourselves to be "in." We had three choices: we could go our separate ways, convert to friendship, or continue on. Next thing I knew, his Match.com account was shut down.

I'd told Bradley about Andrew and what we'd been through within the first few months of dating him, but he didn't meet Andrew until the following December. It was the holidays, and Andrew was in Arizona to see his dad. Not surprisingly, Bradley's response to the details of what Andrew and I had been through was a simple, "Okay." The man is immovable. Again, there was that comforting steadiness. It was just a non-issue, and it became more comfortable for me to talk about what was happening or my concerns or anything that happened in the past. I'd never before felt that freedom, that safe acceptance.

We met Andrew at a restaurant in North Scottsdale. At this point, Andrew was twenty-three, not seven, and yet I was still hesitant for them to meet. Andrew knew I'd been spending time with someone, and by that point I knew that Bradley was going to be a more permanent fixture in my life. I'd been married twice, and Andrew was doing so well. There was no way I was going to do anything that might rock that boat. I needed the timing to be right. I needed it to be easy. Plus, Andrew's edgy. So here I have this guy I'm dating who's a total Boy Scout, and then I have my son, who's…well…an amazing human...but not always a Boy Scout.

Never before had I cared about anything like that. It mattered to me that they liked each other. Nothing could have been worse for me at that moment than if Bradley didn't like my son. And, had that happened, Bradley would have been gone, because my son's not going to be gone. And that would have sucked.

When Andrew gets nervous about something, his edginess shows up in full force. I absolutely love my kid, and when he can bring this particular directness quality into mastery, it's going to be even more powerful. He says exactly what he's thinking, colorful language and all. He has no filter. I love that about him, and yet sometimes he goes too far, which is 100 percent my view and likely not his. For him, it's a "take me as I am…or don't" type of thinking, which I do understand. I'm used to it, but others may not be. He's had this quality since he was younger. If he's getting a negative response from someone, he doesn't retreat. He charges. If you can authentically, yet artfully speak the truth, it's an incredibly powerful tool, but you have to master the "artful" part of that.

I know he was equally nervous about meeting Bradley. I don't think it had as much to do with the fact that it was someone I was dating as it did that he was a solid, very grounded human. You can feel it in his energy. It can be easy to feel like you're not entering into that scenario on solid ground. Because of what Andrew had been through, there was understandably a sense of wanting to prove himself. Plus, he's had two "father" experiences, so this is not exactly a scenario void of emotion. He's always had a desire for acceptance, as all human beings do, and based upon one's past experiences, that desire can be heightened.

Given his innate sensitive, compassionate nature, he's always been very protective of me, and there was a bit of that protective side of him present at the table that day. Over his younger years, he's given me a bazillion bracelets and rings (I still have them all); he used to say he was going to marry me. When he got a bit older, he of course stopped saying he was going to marry me, but the protectiveness didn't dissipate. There's often a special bond between a mom and her son, and with Andrew, that bond has been pretty powerful.

I don't know that Bradley had any nervousness at all going into the meeting. As he always was with me, he was just fully present the entire time, talking about this or that. Another thing I absolutely love about this man is the way he's so present with people. I could literally see him just *being* there with Andrew, in full acceptance of him no matter what. It went as well as it possibly could have gone. The next time they saw one another was actually not until the following Christmas, an entire year later.

We spent that Christmas at my aunt's, and my cousins, Bradley, Andrew, and I decided to start a few traditions. We had matching pajamas and a gift exchange. Andrew had us all cracking up the entire time. He opened each item in his stocking meticulously. This was when Bradley and Andrew developed a fun bond based, unfortunately, on their mutual love for teasing me. If anyone called Bradley *anything* other than my boyfriend, I would react. He was not my husband, my aunt's nephew, my mom's son-in-law, or my bonus parents' bonus son. Being Bradley, he picked up on my discomfort immediately and it became fuel for his reindeer games. So he'd say things like, "Tell Mom I said 'hi!" At first, I was standing my ground, then it just became fun and still is. Once Andrew picked up on the fact that Bradley's teasing was getting under my skin, the two of them became partners in crime. They were wildly entertained all by themselves. They developed a camaraderie, a respect between the two of them.

Finally, after years when the Christmas season was filled with an unmanageable son or hikes by myself, it came with the joy it was always intended to bring. I've learned to be a better partner with Bradley by realizing that you don't get to fine-tune your partner, and if you think that's your job, you're going to be disappointed. I was doing just that, and I've come around. It's not my job to fine-tune my partner unless he's asking me to help him with something. My job is to love him as he is and continue to fine-tune myself.

CHAPTER 25

4/13/16

Neither try to force your feelings nor avoid them...allow your feelings to rise when they do.

Trust your ability to manage then. They will not swallow you whole. They can't. They are present in your being temporarily to offer you something. To teach you something. To show you what matters to you most.

Going through that tsunami year broke things apart so much that I was unwilling to put a single piece back together without certainty that it was a piece I wanted in the puzzle of me. I started from a completely blank slate, and anything that came into my world was allowed in with intention. I chose not to have a television for the purpose of discovering what I would do with my time. I wouldn't buy anything, even something simple, unless I felt that I absolutely wanted to let that thing in. I was constantly asking myself, "What do I really want to bring into my world?" I was in no hurry to figure that out, and yet there was still a restlessness about my life. I had to contend with that, and through simultaneously managing my desire to become mindful alongside my wish to warrior on, I was able to fine-tune what it means to practice being fully present.

In terms of Andrew's recovery during this time, I knew that, no matter what, I simply needed to hold belief. I'd once been a practicing Christian who lived her life according to the faith's principles, and I'm well aware that talking about my current view of these concepts with someone living an active, religiously Christian life would perhaps not go over terribly well. But this has been part of my evolution in the midst of the tsunami. I chose to shift, to open, to confront my beliefs, to consider and sift truths in order to allow myself to be part of the experiment.

When I am in San Diego, I take as many opportunities as I can to walk my favorite beach, La Jolla Shores. I grew up going to this beach when visiting family here, so my walks there give me a feeling of home that is significantly grounding and restorative. I actually crave the experience when it has been too long between visits.

The hikes I take in Arizona seem to help me work things out internally. There is something about climbing, the reaching of the saddle or summit, that proves evolutionary for me. But this particular beach brings me insight, ideas, and inspiration almost every time.

I normally walk north, taking a moment underneath the pier near Scripps. There is something really meditative about watching the waves march forward, one by one, while you look to the opening that seems almost like a doorway to the unknown. From there, I head to the point where most people turn around and climb over the rocks to the area of beach that rarely sees anyone but walkers and surfers. It is my favorite part. That stretch of beach brings another level of solitude with the absence of distractions.

On my way back during a recent walk, as I crossed the rocks and headed down to where I could see the shoreline, I carefully navigated between sand and rocks—my eyes fixed solidly on the ground and my mind fully focused on my next steps—when out of the blue a waist-high wave knocked me off balance. Holding my phone high in the air, I quickly realized that my left foot had collided with a big rock and was probably some degree of bloody. Oddly, I found comfort in the fact that my foot was being bathed in saltwater.

Unexpectedly confronted by high tide, I immediately thought of a book I had read, *The Obstacle Is The Way: The Timeless Art of Turning Trials into Triumph*, by Ryan Holiday. I laughed out loud at my next thought: "Life is a living workshop." I decided to think and feel my way through the experience with absolute calm, being fully present with each step. I thought of the main sections of the book: Perception, Action, and Will.

Strategic™ is my number one strength, and that's where my mind automatically goes with haste. "What is the best possible path for the best possible outcome?" is always the framework I lean on when making decisions.

The cucumber is bitter? Then throw it out.
There are brambles in the path? Then go around.
That's all you need to know.
—Marcus Aurelius

I was in the middle of an area filled with rocks of all shapes and sizes, and because of the high tide, I was not able to see them. Taking a look at the movement and frequency of the waves, I could see that another high wave was likely coming, and I needed to be in motion. Yet I stood there, not moving, as I could not see my next steps.

Sometimes, obstacles will put us in a place of paralysis. With awareness, that frozen moment can be used to develop an obstacle navigation plan. In that moment, it hit me: start moving by feeling your way. I put my right foot forward and felt the ground in front of me. Okay, it's flat, you can step here. Then I stepped with my left foot, but I felt a slope, and a slope usually indicates a nearby rock.

Just then, another wave hit.

Obstacles are negotiable, I thought. I can move around these step by step.

Sometimes, when faced with an obstacle, we feel like we have to have absolute clarity about the solution before we can set any part of it in motion. Often, that belief is the very thing that slows or stops our progress. I have experienced this more than once in my life, but the truth is, you can feel your way through and to the solution, keeping your awareness high and taking that next right step, one step at a time.

With my awareness fixed on the incoming tide, taking small steps with my eyes down and forward, the water receded, and I could see the pattern of rocks for just a moment before the next wave hit. That brief moment allowed me to formulate my navigation plan: feel, and step slowly when you can't see the next step. When you have a clear vision, step faster.

Choosing only to pause and ground my footing when the waves showed the potential to knock me off my feet again, I moved forward through a combination of slow steps and brisk surges and arrived at the "clearing"—the rock-less shore—in just a few minutes.

Sure enough, my foot was a little bloody. But not for one second was I upset about that, because, for me, the entire experience was deeply poignant. I will never look at any obstacle the same way. Instead, there is a new and excited curiosity in me to weather the challenge of discovering which obstacle navigation plan I will choose during each instance that's presented to me.

The most important element of maintaining momentum is to never stop moving.

CHAPTER 26

When you're ascending, the moment you get past the turbulence, when the plane starts to even out and you think, "Oh hell YES!"—that is the moment we do all of this for. The first anniversary of Andrew's sobriety was April 16, 2016. I was several months into my contract with Teague, and it was going beautifully. There were obvious signs of success for both of us, and even still, I was smart enough by that point to fully comprehend that you always hold belief and keep going. We hadn't fully arrived, but we were on the path, we were on the runway, and we were catching speed while feeling our ability and having enough hope to continue to put one foot in front of the other.

We went to a meeting and Andrew shared his story. Watching him make people laugh and be one hundred percent Andrew was amazing. To hear him speak meaningfully and deeply was so impactful. He dropped F-bombs, and it didn't matter. He felt fully accepted, and witnessing this was one of the most moving and memorable moments of my life. We were in the air.

We safely reached a comfortable cruising altitude

around the time of his two-year anniversary. He bought a handsome suit and wanted to surprise me with the absolute fact that he had become a man. In that moment, I felt like, "Okay, I have a whole new level of confidence that we can stay here." The pride, honor, and gratitude I felt were overwhelming. I also remember thinking, "Oh, we are flying now."

There was certainly turbulence between the year one and year two anniversaries. For Andrew, it manifested in his struggle to find his way on a career path. If something happened with a job (as in, he quit or got fired) it rocked my world because I had a cargo hold worth of evidence from his prior job losses that could easily squash my belief. I knew, at that moment, that I had to find a way to ignore that past evidence. I also knew that he was in fear and I knew he had to work his way to solid ground on his own. It was also the perfect opportunity for me to continue the practice of powerful belief. Not just for me but also for him. I have come to understand that our children need to see a solid confidence and belief in them, from us. And when I say solid, I mean that you have to fully believe it. Andrew, like most of us, both had and has a magnificent bullshit radar.

I wanted to show the change. I'd never had a suit and I wanted one. It represented something as simple as "I can buy a suit now." I wanted my mom to see me in a suit. It was more that I wanted to wear the suit for dinner with my mom, than I did for the meeting. I wanted to take her to a nice dinner. I told her to dress up and pick out her dress so that we would match. I knew it would touch her heart and I wanted to have a suit that was mine for events like funerals. I started shopping, found a tailor, started asking questions, and piecing it together over time because I couldn't afford it all at once and I wanted it to be nice.

I got the shirt and the bowties first. Then I picked out a gray suit and I went to Saks Off Fifth and found Michael Kors suit that was originally $2600 for $600. Later I got a belt and shoes to match. I spent a little from each paycheck to put it all together. It took about two months to get it all together.

Cruising altitude on my end was felt in the progress I was feeling professionally. There was the amazing experience of signing my first large contract with a corporate client—and then believing that it wasn't just a fluke. I believed that all the progress was made for a reason, and I understood that I could believe for even more and take the next step.

I had a client in Northern California, and during one of my many drives there from Arizona, I was thinking about the fact that one client really wasn't enough to justify the amount of travel I was doing. I believe in the high value of face-to-face meetings, so I didn't want to convert our meetings to phone or even video conference. However, I felt like I needed to find just one more client—even if only a small one—in Northern California to justify the constant back-and-forth trips. So that's exactly what I said I desired: one more client in Northern California. Unsure as to exactly how that was going to work out, I continued driving. I kid you not, the next week I got an introduction that I *did not* ask for from Byron Johnson of Teague Insurance to a company in Northern California, and the work they needed would take exactly as long as the contract that I had with my other Northern California-based client.

After that experience, I thought, "Okay, *now* what do I desire?" I'm able to get super clear on what I desire, but when it comes to the pieces I can't control, I simply trust. I'm blessed to have hindsight and be able to remind myself that if it happened before, it can happen again (and again). We all have the opportunity to dance in that knowing, and when you look back, you can easily see that you didn't understand then, but you do now. You see how the experiences have carried you along and how one thing turned into something else you didn't initially envision. Because of that knowing, I can trust that whatever is happening is happening for my greater good and the greater good of others.

While I've mentioned hindsight many times (because I believe it's completely natural for us to employ it), I also have come to understand that when we can truly be in a level of awareness—a true practice of presence—and practicing that *in*, the need for hindsight is minimized. You can actively participate in the unfolding of a situation in a different way. Sometimes, what we say isn't what we truly feel. Our thoughts, words, and actions express different feelings. It is when they all align that we have found the absolute depth of our truth. The more time we take to let our real—not fear-based—thoughts settle into our hearts and move from that place, the more authentic we become. When a situation is approached in this way, there won't be the same need to later reflect upon it. Wholehearted living doesn't really begin until we can begin living from this place.

My greatest fear when branching out from that first client was, without doubt, *What if none of it works? What if there are no results and everybody says, "This hasn't helped us." What if it all falls apart and I'm left with nothing.* I had to hope that the success of my work with my first major client wasn't simply a fluke! One of my strongest beliefs is around the power of working from our personal tribe. Just a few months before this time I had reached out to a previous boss of mine, Ken Kirk, who is a man and leader I respect. I remember sharing with him my concerns about how to prove results in a quantifiable way. He basically told me that all I had to do was qualify, not quantity. That gave me yet another level of confidence.

I believe that if you show up a certain way for people, consistently focused on how to bring value, it's very easy for them to lead you or refer you into other organizations. This is the beauty of seeing the tribe you've built working for you. One of those people was a dear friend of mine, Taylor Boyd. I met him in the early years of my insurance career, and at a lunch meeting I remember sharing with him that I had figured out who my ideal client was. To which he responded, "I know who you need to meet." He persistently made the request to introduce us.

So far, just about every business I've worked with has recommended me to another business they work with. Clients simply say, "You need to meet Deborah; you need to work with her." For that I am incredibly grateful. I've had to trust the process of intentional, organic growth. This also included my commitment to vigorously pursue my own growth, because part of my growth helped me to come alongside others in *their* growth. I knew I needed to take action in order to get where I wanted to go while simultaneously trusting that things were coming together. That was the critical allowance piece—I allowed for the unfolding and didn't need to control it in order for it to show up exactly the way I thought it needed to. I recognized that I could be a part of the creative process and see how things came to life, which is one of the coolest methods available to us. The more evidence you begin to see in your life of this process truly working, the easier it is to believe in it.

The expectation of a specific outcome is one of our biggest obstacles. We mess up by creating a conclusion that has not yet been written. In my view and experience, when you can let go of *how* it unfolds and, instead, just get into motion, take action, and pay attention, you are truly in the dance of creation.

When two people are both being challenged in a situation such as this, it can be easy for a level of enablement to ensue. We were able to avoid that because, even in the difficult moments, we just navigated and continued to encourage each other to put one foot forward. He was building his tribe, and I was building mine. It was invigorating.

If he and I had a conflict and there was intensity or harshness in communication through tone or chosen words—usually brought on by a loss of control or frustration for Andrew—we'd stop. If the conversation turned to ineffective or unloving, we'd stop. Andrew would always be the one to re-engage and say, "Mom, I'm sorry. I was an asshole. This is what was happening." He's learned those skills through the program he's worked. I no longer worry *When we will talk again?* because, while it used to be much harder, I look back upon my life for evidence of what will transpire, as Sheila taught me to do. The evidence has shown me that he will circle back when he's ready. I shift gears because I can't stay in that energy; I have to move into a different energy. My life is thankfully quite busy, which makes it easier for me to make that necessary shift.

Fierce love requires a responsibility to self. You must recognize what your thought process is doing to you in the moment it's doing it. If you have a relationship where there's discontent for any reason at any point in time, and you can recognize that you don't have control over what's happening, to continue to obsess and replay the conversation to try to figure it out isn't acting in faith or having fierce self-love. That incessant dialogue is not healthy for anyone. Ever. I know, I used to entertain it far too often. Create some space, let it go, be in self-love, restore, then you can look at the situation more objectively. With practice, everyone can learn to let logic lie down on top of your emotion. Or let emotion come to meet one's logic. It is the colorful dance between heart and head. Let your feelings be present. Don't deny them. Don't logic them away. But don't let them dominate. Let logic and feelings marry one another. Let your truth be your truth, but don't let things get out of control or make them any bigger than they are. We are *really* good at that as human beings, at the drama of it all. But, in the end, it hurts us to be in a constant state of infusing our life situations with drama.

Whenever there is a lack of comfort within oneself, that agitation wants to be satisfied. One wants attention and connection, so they believe that if they bring some drama to the moment, they can get the comfort that they seek. The more that you become solid with your own company and content in your own skin, and the more you apply principles of genuinely loving yourself, the less you will have a need for drama, which never fully brings the comfort that's sought. So it's repeated. The need for drama can be an addiction of its own.

Even after everything that's happened in my life, I'm still committed to my own personal and professional growth. Once I complete a flight that maxes out at 38,000 feet, my next question is, "How do I make it to 40,000 feet?" We're all taking flight all the time. Parts of your previous flights perhaps weren't fun, but they gave you new tools. Be aware of the point of departure for your next-level flight so you can be prepared to leave. But, at the same time, don't allow your delay, your doubts, your worry about the things that can slow you down to take hold. Simply gathering flights is no different from simply gathering knowledge if there is no application of anything learned within them.

However, it's also about more than looking for the next learning experience, accomplishment, or giving opportunity. It's important to be thoughtful about and available for what's next. It's not as simple as asking, "What's next? I'm ready to attack everything I possibly can." The intentional selection from the soul in terms of what's next matters, and that requires slowing oneself down enough to hear what the soul has to say. It requires a sifting of sorts. I have allowed myself a greater degree of ease in moving through everything. I have let go of the demand I internally felt for how I do anything. I have given myself enough grace to be able to sift and discover the gems while leaving the sand. We've got to become incredible sifters for ourselves, and we truly need to be better sifters for each other.

CHAPTER 27

8/4/16

When I reside in the sea of my own calm...I see.

It is only my expectations that create unwanted feelings... these feelings of being unsafe.

I am always safe. I am always learning. I am always growing...and in all relationships I am always becoming more conscious...

Somewhere along the way, I started to notice that listening to people—really, truly observantly listening to them as though you are sharing energetic space—has profound results. As I moved along in my life and interacted with others, I've learned about myself through my own listening process, but I also began to see the value of honing my listening skills to include observing the moment I was in.

It's not about just the words that someone is saying. It's about everything around those words: their physical mannerisms, their energy, their facial expressions, the things that they're not saying, the way they hesitate, the way their voice changes. To listen observantly is to see the whole person. The whole moment. What is or isn't needed. It's not about simply listening. Further, we can listen observantly to life. We can listen observantly to our inner spirit. We can be so present that we can see a moment's true meaning. It's a level of connection with yourself and humanity wherein you connect with the fact that what's truly happening is deep and rooted and meaningful. It's the very essence of a single moment, and it's all that matters. I can hear someone say sixteen things and then get right to the core of what they're really expressing. But I must truly hear them first, not assume I know what they are going to say. When you can do that with another human being, they genuinely feel heard, understood, and maybe even seen in a way that they've not yet seen themselves. It allows them to see their reflection in your reception of them. Sometimes, you see a light come on, and the person says, "Ohmigod, yes!" as though they suddenly see themselves in a new way.

The day that Andrew was arrested in front of me, I recognized that my son was being arrested and I needed to listen observantly, to be fully aware of myself in that moment so as not to be in a state of panic or blame or anger. I needed to simply stay steady and observe what was happening. I observed the officers, their words and their non-verbal communication. I observed the simple flow of events. I heard my son, saw his face, knew he was scared, and knew that what I was seeing was the purest, most authentic piece of him in that moment. I allowed myself to be in a space where I was able to simply be the love, strength, and resolve that I needed to be. I could see that all he needed in that moment was my love and to know that I was right there. He also needed to know it was his situation to solve. I observed from all angles in order to understand what was happening both around and within me. The same observant listening happened during that long night when Andrew was in the hospital, and I am beyond grateful to have had the presence of being necessary to engage it.

Listening observantly is having a level of presence that's not the easiest to describe. It's meditative, in a sense. If I speak in terms of my romantic relationship, sometimes Bradley and I will be talking to each other about something, and maybe the conversation is a bit heated. Perhaps, because of his past experience, or the stress of the moment, he'll have a little bit of an edgy reaction to my words. It would be perfectly natural for me to edge right back, and I'm definitely not saying that I've never done that!

A couple of summers ago, we were in Houston for his high school reunion, and were having an amazing time. We went to a restaurant for lunch, and we ordered a drink that was supposed to be a peach Bellini, but it was made with rum, and it was unbelievably strong. I hadn't even finished one—which is supposed to be made with peach puree and champagne—and I was completely toasted.

We were having a conversation about how to counsel Andrew as it related to some business topic, and I said something to which he responded with what I received as a bit of an attitude. The conversation began to get intense, and he got frustrated. He stood up to leave, and my stubbornness kicked in. After all, I wasn't finished with my drink! He told me to come to the car, and I said that I'd come when I was ready. Bradley commented via text that if I wasn't ready by a certain time, I could take Uber. So that's what I ended up doing. I took Uber to the airport, and he met me there. It was incredibly childish behavior on both of our parts, and at the time, I was full of righteous sass.

Fast-forward to the moment it came time to have a conversation about this incident. I realized that when he said I could leave the restaurant with him or take an Uber to the airport, my mindset was one of "Don't make threats; I'll call your bluff." He was thinking the exact same thing by suggesting that I take an Uber! As we began to discuss the he-said-she-said details, I realized that we were getting absolutely nowhere. The conversation was supposed to be about resolution, and as I observed his body language, communication style, and the words he used, I recognized that something about my behavior that day in the restaurant in

Houston had made him angry. His behavior that day wasn't normal either, and he was exhibiting a similar energy as we recounted the event. I could see in his countenance that there was more to it than what he was saying.

I said, "I feel like there is something else here." After a pause, he was able to see that one of his frustrations with me is my stubbornness, so in resistance to that, he suggested that I take an Uber. As we explored further, I wondered if there was any other way that my stubbornness shows up to him, and he said that he wishes I could let go of my past. I was holding onto self-protection and he could feel it. And, by the way, he was right.

I was in no condition while stubbornly finishing my Bellini to ask, "How is this about more than what he is saying? What else is here? What does this moment need" There is a roaring speed that we as humans can get into, and we start to argumentatively dialogue and unload. You have to slow yourself down enough to make the conversation you're having constructive and productive and to create the outcome you want. Had I not paid attention to his facial expressions and the nuance of his energy while we were reflecting, and had I not genuinely wanted to know more, we wouldn't have gotten to clarity. I initially perceived his reaction in the restaurant as a divisive one, when in fact his frustration was coming from a deep desire to come together.

When I'm in a professional environment, sitting across the table from someone in a sales situation, I would of course like them to want to do business with me. Because we're in the beginning of our business relationship, I might naturally want to tell them all the great reasons why they should want to do business with me. But, to listen observantly is to ask certain questions and then watch everything that's happening in terms of the other person's response. I have to be fully present to feel someone's energy, to hear their answers, to gauge their tone, to feel their movement. I will learn everything I need to know by paying attention from deep as well as wide angles, and it's an ability everyone can cultivate.

As a leader, my aim is to motivate and inspire, and in this capacity there are problems that I need to solve. Somebody might come into my office, frustrated with a coworker. If I simply attach to what is being said, I'll never truly help them solve anything. I always have to be mindful of what's being said as well as what isn't being said—what's underneath it all and where our opportunity to create progression lies so that we don't end up revisiting the issue a week, month, or year later. Whether in their personal or professional lives, most people want a richness in relationships that can progress.

My clients can be themselves with me no matter what because I am fully present with both them and myself. I don't come from a place of judgement. I'm not here to make anyone wrong. I'm here to hear someone, to receive them, to help them sift, to consider seeing from a different lens and to see where we can adjust an approach that allows us/them to rise up.

We can't grow from a place we're pretending to live. We can only grow from the place where we actually live. If I'm pretending, I'm downfield. That's not real, rooted, or grounded. I can't even make sense of where I should be because all I know is that I'm here and I missed the experiences that would have prepared me for that place. The difference between acting as if and believing as if is also cellular.

Practicing presence and listening observantly are intertwined. I am fully present with myself, present in my own being—not just present in this room at the table. I can ground down to where I am right now as a person interacting, what it is that I really desire, and where it is that I wish to go. It's not just about being in the room. It's being so fully connected to my mind, body, spirit, and emotion that I truly see everything that is there for me. Being fully present is not missing a thing. It's meditative but alert.

There was a good part of my life during which I felt almost like I was floating above my own being, like I wasn't fully connected to myself. I would have an after-the-fact feeling, almost like a realization that I wouldn't have missed something if I hadn't been distracted. There was just a disconnect, and maybe the disconnect was actually me coming to the realization that practicing presence represents a deep inner desire to be connected to myself, to have a true visceral awareness of who I am and of what value I bring. I've always understood that the latter part of that isn't about only me. It's also about every other person I connect with. At some point, I came to understand that I can't fully be there for somebody else unless I'm in my own fullness, and what the hell actually is that?

Recently, Bradley and I were driving, and I was telling him that I was feeling really good about my growth. There is a woman at our gym who we'd both been noticing. She has a gorgeous running stride and the stereotypically toned runner's body, and he notices these things in great detail. There was a time when my insecurities might have made the fact that he takes notice mean something, but on this particular day, I didn't care. I said, "I feel like I've progressed. I feel like I've come to a good place, because this would have bothered me before and put me into comparison mode."

Less than an hour later, that very same woman was our cashier at Lowe's. It was like the universe was saying, "Here it is, in your face, Deborah. Are you really not bothered?" And I wasn't.

CHAPTER 28

1/1/2017

You plant the seeds; they choose where they water. Watching Andrew evolve has been the most amazing feeling. Its gift is so much more rewarding because of all we have come through.

When you become a parent, you want to throw everything you have at it. Why? Because there's an investment window, and when it closes, your influence and role change. So you want to capitalize on every opportunity to seed. I took every conscious opportunity to seed plant. And I am loving watching his conscious and subconscious selection of what feels right for him.

Coming up on Andrew's three-year sobriety birthday, he was a bit distant. I knew something was up, but it felt good not to feel the way I used to. The worry I felt by this point could be likened to the way I suspect most parents feel concern and genuine caring for their children—not twisted into knots by panic-laced fear. That's how I used to feel when he went dark for days or when the phone rang in the middle of the night. Now, I have the knowledge that he has developed his own way of navigating life.

Equipping our kids is vital. One thing I wish I would have done earlier was to put him in situations in which he had to make decisions so that I could engage him through questions in order to help him find his own way to a healthy personal choice. I would have done that a little bit differently had I had even a semblance of an idea of where we were headed. The specific kind of decision he would have been making itself didn't really matter; flexing the decision-making muscle is what was critical. We didn't make every decision for him; he was actually quite the captain of his own ship, hence his negotiation skills. But those negotiation skills are now working in his favor, which is miraculous to observe. Perhaps there are ways we could have helped him learn that earlier, and perhaps there are not.

I'm here, in this place, and it's good. It's also so incredibly important to stay in humility, to stay in gratitude, to stay in appreciation for what is right now. This is something that Andrew and I both deeply understand. Not only does that understanding affect my present moment, it also affects my future moment. Appreciation is an energy, and through practice of it, I came to realize that, first of all, I absolutely one hundred percent believe that thoughts are things. I believe that we manifest through the concentration of what we're projecting our thoughts onto. I also believe we manifest with thoughts, words, and energy. The energy of appreciation has a power all its own, and the ability to stay in the presence of appreciation is one I've come to know through practice.

Life happens, and stuff is going to happen, and I know that the path is not sheer bliss from this point forward. I'm fully aware of that fact. And it's okay, because what I do by allowing in the fear of the unknown or fear of another shoe ready to drop is fragment or minimize the amazing moment that I'm in, and I'm not willing to rob myself or anybody in my life of the fullness of each moment because I am fearful of what's going to come.

I've learned to trust that I have within me whatever it is I need in order to handle whatever it is that will be presented, and that whatever presents itself is there for my gain, even if it's terribly hard. It's not that my thoughts never dance with fear. If I said that were true, it would be a big bunch of bullshit. It would be a big bunch of bullshit if anybody said it was true in their life. I've simply learned not to allow those fears enter in and take over. They try to dance with me, and I have to remind myself (and them) that they're not my dance partner anymore.

It's a work to be present. It's a work to stay in joy like energy. It takes awareness, attention, and focus. As someone who used to employ worst-case-scenario thinking, I didn't come to fully understand how truly ineffective worst-case scenario thinking is until the past 9 years.

There are steps between one perspective and the other. There's first the "What's the worst-case scenario and how can I deal with it so that I can make it through?" perspective, and then somewhere after that the perspective shifts to "I can handle it because I'm not dead." At a point, I began to wonder, Why don't I think more often in terms of best possible outcome? I call this BPO thinking. That feels way better. It's a miraculous moment when you come to the realization that you're affecting your own energy and thereby your own experience and outcome by the way you focus on something. If I say, "I've navigated this far, so I know I can handle what comes" or ask, "What's the best outcome?" I can think in terms of what that looks like and how I head in that direction. That's also an evolution. My grandmother used to say to me, "There is power in the spoken word." As a child, those felt like mere words. If thoughts actually become things and there is power in spoken words, I'll use that knowledge to my advantage. Anything that happens once can happen again. If you can open the door once, you can open it again.

We all, as human beings, go through a graduated evolution wherein there's opportunity for us to become open to new awareness and what I would consider to be universal laws. For instance, the notion that if you can do it once you can do it again is a universal law. It's a structural aspect of the human existence. Once you've proven to yourself that something is possible, you begin to wonder where else that philosophy can be applied. We come to different levels of this through our experiences. It's a progression of our human evolution, and how much we engage in it determines how we choose to look at it and how far we go.

By this thinking, it now makes sense to me that Julie and I could both be raised in the same place by the same parents, and I'd think, "I can't do that" and "She has more gift than I do." But also, "Wait a minute; that's bullshit."

"Wait a minute" has been a transformative principle for me. It spurred me to disprove those things I believed (or believe) to be true. These days, what I ask is, *What shall we create?* I believe with every fiber in my being that we are in creation every single day, and there's no limit to that. We just can't necessarily control the timing, nor every detail.

Active creation requires that I actually step in. That's the bravery that's required, the courage to act, regardless of what other action is necessary. The first time, or the first couple of times, you don't necessarily know that you have to step in, so it's like something almost teases you. You continue to shorten the timeline between determining what you want to create and experiencing the manifesting of it in reality because you're learning faith, action, and trust, on repeat. That's the power that comes from understanding the dance between action and allowance. Action and allowance must co-exist. What's simultaneously interesting and challenging about getting to this point in the journey is that the two seem to be in conflict. They don't seem like they could co-exist, and yet they must in order to be in the active state of creation. If you drive with only your logical brain, you won't be able to get past that point.

I'm not interested in seeing what someone else does merely to copy them. I want to see what they do and then do it in my own way so that I can learn what the experience has for me. I once attended a scrapbooking class wherein every other participant did almost exactly what the instructor showed them, while I did my own thing. They were perplexed as to why I would do this, but I had recognized how important it is to let an experience have its creative way with me.

My tendency long ago was to go to worst-case-scenario thinking. I chose to go after some re-training in order to shift to best-possible-outcome (BPO) thinking. I made up that descriptor, but it works, and I often incorporate it into my work with others. I've practiced BPO thinking since my early thirties, and in the beginning, I was okay at it. But I really learned how to practice it, implement it, and benefit from it when I came to understand that I was actually creating through my thinking and resulting energy. It's more than visualization. It's the power of standing in belief of one's vision with full detachment, which can sound kind of contrary, but it's quite the opposite. Full detachment is the presence and the power of faith.

The art of manifestation requires both clarity of desire and absolute non-attachment to the unfolding. Being attached to the way you think things will go is what you must detach from. I did the work. I got the training. Now I have to see how it will unfold. I need to have fun with it. I need to change the framework around the experience; if I'm insistent that the path unfolds in only one way, I'm likely going to be disappointed. Creativity can't come in when we're rigid. If, on the other hand, I can be playful and flexible and love the unfolding, it will all evolve beautifully in both unexpected and magical ways.

I don't think about what life would have been like had Julie not passed away, had I not experienced some not-so-great relationships, had I not been raised by an alcoholic, had Andrew not gone through what he's gone through, had I not also experienced all of the other happenings that are swamp-like in nature. I have incredible gratitude for it all, and I would do it again, as excruciating as it was. It allowed me to be refined by fire, and we don't get to these amazing moments where we are solidly rooted without going through things that refine us. That's what unfathomable experiences do to us. If you could look at yourself as a color and then have an experience, after which you'd see that new colors had been introduced, pretty soon there would be a blending, a variety of beautiful, vibrant colors. You become your own version of a rainbow. Who wants to be all purple?

People with few challenging experiences in life can have a kind of clean energy. No one wants to invite difficulties, but don't push away from them. On the surface, the human frame looks like a nice pretty package. But when you take away that frame, the soul of a person who's gone through a lot is much more colorful and vibrant for it, most of the time anyway. There are people who go through the same tragic experiences very differently. The colors they take on are not vibrant. The way they allow themselves to be weighed down by the experiences instead of letting themselves move through them and then letting them go, leaving them behind. There are stories that end in despair and devastation and depression. Their light dims, whereas when you make a different choice, light expands. And what is key is to continue to make the choices that expand and enhance the brilliance of your light.

I've observed Andrew working through this state of being and evolution as well. I've heard him say things sprinkled with worst-case-scenario dust, and I simply observe it. I don't correct him at all. My approach is right for me. He's got to come to his reframing on his own. That doesn't mean that I can't plant considerations in just such a way, and I am available for those opportunities, but I'm not going to tell him that the framework he's using to deal with life right now is not right. He is on his own growth path. That's not for me to do. I must only love him exactly where he is.

I have also learned that my son does not need me to parent him. What he needs is more of a sounding board, a supporter, and an unwavering source of belief. As parents, we each have an internal and almost automatic go-to in terms of our "parenting response." And it is our job to learn how to morph into a different mode so that the now-adults we brought in can walk their own road, make their own way, create their own life. They will make mistakes, have victories, and learn. Just as we did.

Today, Andrew lives in an apartment with a friend who is also sober. He's been fully responsible for the making of his own life for quite a while. April 16, 2020 will mark five years of sobriety. He vapes, and the nicotine is something he's addicted to, but when you weigh that out against, oh I don't know, heroin, I'm okay with it. He's edgy. He has tattoos. He's himself. I can hear it when I'm on the phone with him. He's happy, and he's got entrepreneur blood in him, a ton of ideas and a lot of exuberance. He's learning how to navigate the business world, and he feels great about it all. He also has to navigate fears now and then, and he has a tribe of friends, a process, and a program he leans on for that.

I was curious as to how Andrew would speak to a "turning point" in his recovery journey, so we spoke about that one day.

There wasn't one big turning point. My life just gradually got better as I continued to do the right thing to the best of my abilities. There wasn't a distinct shift; it was daily micro-shifts of "I'm not going to do that."

When I was thirty days sober, I didn't have any money. I didn't want to ask my parents for money because I'd taken enough from them already. I went to the gas station and I went to steal a bag of chips and as I was walking out, I just couldn't do it. I turned around, put them back, and walked out. I didn't say anything to anyone; I just realized that if I did the right thing, as cliché as it sounds, the right things would continue to happen.

I've been scared plenty of times while in sobriety. I've been fired from jobs, I've had all sorts of shit happen, but I've never gone hungry and I've never not had a roof over my head. In sobriety, the important thing is to stay grateful, especially for the small things, the things we often take for granted. I've been without food. I've been without shelter. So it's easy for me to appreciate the small things. When you're grateful for the small, you can be grateful for the big, You can't just jump to the big stuff.

Gratitude for the small things is the key to everything.

The universe won't give me more things if I don't show through action that I'm grateful for the current things I have. The universe thrives on gratitude. One thing I was told that took me a while to understand is that gratitude is an action word. You can't just say, "I'm grateful for..." You have to show gratitude. I can't just say I'm grateful for my car; I have to show it by keeping it clean and washing it and paying attention to polishing the tires. There's a homeless guy to whom I give $20 each time I see him. He's the nicest guy I've ever met. He's happier than ever, and he doesn't use drugs or alcohol. He's just in a situation he can't get out of. But he's so incredibly grateful for everything—even for his "new" shoes (that are far from new).

I have moments, frequently, where I'm overwhelmed with gratitude. For example, when I'm driving in my nice car to work in Southern California and I look around at my car and my surroundings and I'll start tearing up. It's not that I don't think I deserve it; it's almost as though I won the lottery. I don't feel like I can take credit for any of it. Just through one thing after another, God was just preparing me and taking me to the next level. For the most part, my life only continues to get better and better and better.

CHAPTER 29

Not too long ago, I was in search of a new tool to use with my clients. I couldn't find quite what I was looking for until, one day, I came across an amazing game called The Coaching Game. I was immediately engaged. Not long after, I signed up for the Points of You™ certification program that took place in Half Moon Bay, California. It was a five day, fabulous—yet very intense—all day, all night experience shared with twenty other beautiful souls from all over the world. Through this experience I came to realize there was a bit of subtle shame and unforgiveness I needed to release. I also realized that it was myself I needed to forgive. It was also the place my commitment to write this book was made.

Toward the end of the week we had an amazing experience where we arose at sunrise and walked in silence together toward the ocean. We were instructed to pick up something along the way and imagine whatever it was that we needed to let go of flowing into that item. I picked up a thick, short stick. Walking toward the beach as I held this stick in my hand, I thought over the whole of my experiences. I began to be more loving in my thoughts.

We stood arm in arm several yards from the shoreline, and one at a time we had our individual moments. When it was my turn, I had an overwhelming feeling of support from these strangers I had so quickly grown close to. As I walked close to the water, I thought about how subtly I had been unloving to myself, and with a gut-deep shout, with everything in me, I threw the stick in the ocean. The experience was indescribably powerful, and as I returned to this new beloved tribe, I felt so much lighter.

No matter who you are, if you have a loved one—especially if it is your child—who falls into an unhealthy addiction of some kind, you will eventually come to a point where you consciously or subconsciously blame yourself in a variety of ways. Questions such as "What could I have done differently, better?", "Why didn't I see it sooner?", "Did I do enough?", and "Did I do too much?" will echo in the recesses of your mind. What I want you to claim right here and now is this truth: You did your very best. Blaming yourself is of no value to you. Get wholly honest with yourself, own what you own, and forgive yourself. Hold your head high. There is no shame needed here.

Anything can happen to anyone at any time. There are people who right now think, "Not my kid; this won't happen to us." And *this* could be defined by many different things. I caution you, because I too thought that. I was wrong. Don't let yourself get so caught up in your ego or righteousness that you miss what might be right in front of you. Equally, I caution you from judging your neighbor for whatever tragedy may fall into their life. Compassion is our only worthy response.

Looking back, I recognize that each challenging stage of my life has placed me first in the swamp, then in the desert, and finally, at the leading edge of the runway. In order to most effectively navigate each, I had to remain steadfast in my pursuit of flight. It's in absorbing and appreciating the unique aspects of the *entire* flight—from the sludge-filled trek through the swamp to the arid and visceral emptiness of the desert to the runway to takeoff to landing—that the real beauty of this life becomes available to each of us.

You make it to the runway. You catch speed. You have liftoff. You get to a comfortable cruising altitude. And then you sit back in your chair with the idea that the goal is simply to stay there. But it's not. Cruising altitude is not a permanent state of being, nor is it meant to be. When I was younger, I thought that it was. I truly believed—as many of us do—that we eventually get to cruising altitude and just hang out there, admiring the clouds and the storm in the distance and the complimentary peanuts.

What *is* true about cruising altitude is that it's found inside moments. There is an ebb and a flow to it. It's present during the moments when we feel like,

"Okay, I'm on the right track." It's present during the moments of connection and progression. It's even present within the sweet moments of victory. But it isn't a perpetual state, just as no flight lasts forever. There's always going to be another swamp, another desert, another runway, another takeoff, another climb, another cruising altitude, another landing. Where we screw ourselves up is in believing that we should consistently live at cruising altitude. The joy is found in every aspect of the flight, from beginning to end. And again. And again. Everything you gain from each trudge through the swamp, crawl through the desert, and, finally, liftoff into flight stays with you and prepares you better for the next.

There were many moments during Andrew's rise when he struggled. There were many moments during my rise when *I* struggled. But the conviction to "stick and stay and go from here" was ever-present for both of us. We both continued to make more powerful decisions that would move us forward. We have a beautiful relationship wherein we share all of our moments—the good, the great, the godawful. Each time one of us had a victory, it fueled the other, and that feeling of rising together became so motivating. When one of us was doing well, we both celebrated, even if only in our hearts. When one was struggling, it outright affected the other, but we would rally together through the power of encouragement. That's the level of soul connection we share, and we got to realize what that kind of soul connection actually looks like by experiencing it all together, side by side.

I aim to be, and I am, freely forgiving. Mostly because I truly understand our human nature and I don't—or do my very best not to—make people wrong for their humanness. After all, it's the structure we were given from which to move, grow, and experience.

But our human nature and our character are mutually exclusive. Our human nature isn't our values. It isn't our beliefs. Instead, these are things we continuously choose in the evolution of our being, our soul. Our choices and priorities guide the shaping of both who we are and who we become.

It takes conscious awareness and desire to be fully in the wholehearted pursuit of your soul. It takes fierce, introspective honesty. You choose the paths, the perceptions, and the lessons through either conscious or unconscious awareness. The most powerful growth comes from conscious selection.

Standing at a crossroads, which path will you choose? What will each bring you in terms of lessons, in terms of emotion, experience, evolution? Even if a road shows you at its point of entry that it will bring to you soul-tearing growth, remember that you often get to choose it, all of it—the good and the not so pleasant.

In fact, we should celebrate the coming out of the swamp each and every time we do. For God's sake, doing so is a damn accomplishment, in and of itself, every single time, almost as if you walk out and say to yourself, "Swamp twenty-five, I made it out! *Booya!*" with a fist pump to the sky.

In the swamp, the desert, the flight, and landing, the confident declaration of "And again," we find the determination to powerfully navigate life by finding the vine of power in any circumstance—the vine that we can take to the next thing. This isn't about finding a silver lining. Seeing the positive in a situation is important, but what I'm referring to is being willing to stand and observe both the light and the dark and pulling from them the vine of power that allows us to powerfully navigate life.

One of the best things we can do with our emotions is let them move through us. Feel them, look at them, and then let them go (well, the ones that don't serve us). It is important to note that, for some people, that process takes longer than it does for others. And the depth or gravity of emotion is a critical factor when it comes to running it through. The power in personal strength comes when both logic and emotion can be accessed simultaneously, whether one is navigating an emotional situation or a logical endeavor.

No matter if I'm negotiating a situation with my son, my ex-husband(s), my partner, my friend, my coworker, my colleague, my client, or a stranger at the post office, these are my principles.

From a more powerful perspective, you go through

the swamp and the desert because you want to ultimately take flight. It's the road to the runway. Of course there are moments when you think, "Really? Does *this* have to be part of it?" But the magic is in the whole flight. There is real beauty on the road to the runway, even if it's through the swamp or the desert. There is real beauty in the runway itself and the feeling of catching speed. And there is real beauty in the takeoff, the cruising altitude, the turbulence, the landing, and the preparation for the next flight. I have been in fierce pursuit of flight my entire life.

The moment you land isn't the end of the journey. Another life situation to navigate is inevitable. Situation, swamp, desert, runway. You firmly plant your feet on the runway. You stare off at the horizon with steadfast resolve and reverential enthusiasm, not completely sure what's coming next.

And you say to the cosmos, "And again."

About the Author

Deborah G. Edwards is an award-winning corporate development expert. She's served as an entrepreneur, business owner, Sales AVP, Division Manager for an MGA, and more. Throughout her more than 30-year career, she developed a passion for helping others achieve success in sales, leadership, and personal growth.

Now, as a Gallup Certified Strengths Coach, Points Of You® Master & Certified Trainer, and speaker, Deborah pours her breadth of experience and passion for people into training others. She helps her clients harness their strengths, celebrate their uniqueness, and develop their innate leadership abilities to improve professional success and promote personal growth.

www.deborahgedwards.com

Acknowledgements

First and foremost, to God and the godly universe, thank you for the multitude of ways you show up in the world. Your very existence is manna to my soul.

To those who have gone before me, who have set the example—good and bad—for myself and for others, thank you for being the forerunners of our lives.

To my son, Andrew Conner Jurek. I love you with a depth that words cannot adequately describe. I adore your absolute resolve to be you, in full authenticity. I am extraordinarily grateful to have walked and sometimes crawled with you along this path, both up and down. Your wit, quick thinking, humor, determination, and vigor have added loads of zest to my life. You are meant to make a difference in the lives of many, my son. You are courageous, unique, and a conqueror! Thank you for making me your mother!

To Bradley Walker, thank you for the beautiful way your love came into my life. Thank you for being the partner I have always craved. Thank you for the way you hold such amazing awareness of me, for your steady loving energy, for your sharp intellect that always keeps me interested, for the way you listen so observantly to me, and for the way you open your mind and heart to me. For laughing with me in the silly moments and simply holding me when my tears flow. You are, without question, my knight in shining armor and the love of my life.

To my mother, Rita Suthers. Your love, support, resilience, and determination to find your own happiness, even in some of life's darkest moments, have been and continue to be poignant examples for me. You are supportive and loving, and were sometimes tough on me in the moments I needed you to be. I truly felt—and still feel—a love and support from you for Andrew that could (almost) match mine. Thank you for the gift of life, and for your never-ending love. Thank you for never giving up. Thank you for your tender heart. I love you, Mama.

To my father in heaven, Don Gerard. It is complex, the way your life and your way of living impacted me. Your love was felt with almost equal measure to your fierceness. Your wisdom and voice, I truly miss. You built within me a desire for excellence and a rock-solid determination that has served me well. Thank you for always letting me be your little project buddy. Thank you for your heart. Thank you for your humanness.

To my aunt and uncle, Ed and Ann Cernin. Throughout my life you set for me the example of commitment, of love. You stood up for me, counseled me, and loved me. Your home was always open to me. So many holidays and summers were shared there. You labeled me "like a daughter," and your presence in my life was the feeling of family. To Scott, Jill, Bob, Jacqui, Ben, Nick, Cindi, Todd, Madison, Kate, Kaylie, Joe, Joe Jr., little Miss Rosalie, and little Mr. Graham, you are the constant. Sprinkled throughout my entire life are memories with you. I love the unquestionable truth that we show up, and I love you all very much.

To my bonus parents, Jean and Al Batson, you are the unexpected blessing that not everyone gets. You took me in without hesitation and gave me a very safe and soft place to land when I was at my weakest point in life. I always felt welcome. I always felt loved. You have listened, shared advice, and laughed a million laughs with me. You breathed breath into me. The relationship we built through this experience has added abundantly to my life. 2012 was a healing year for me, in part because of both of you. You are both incredibly special people. Thank you for being my bonus parents. I love you so very much.

To Elizabeth Lyons, partnering with you to create the book has been a fabulous experience. You have been a blessing every step of the way, from the first question of "What if it only impacts one person, do you still want to do it?", which put me immediately in the right mindset, to your calming of my fears in the nerve-filled moments along the way, to the magic you added with your artful way with words. You are more than an editor, more than a ghostwriter, you are a true creative partner. You my friend, are a special kind of wonderful. Thank you!

To Lisa Snyder, your friendship throughout the years is one of my life's greatest blessings. Your support and never-ending love has, in so many moments, given me a strength I needed to take the next step. Thank you for always truly seeing Andrew and for your gorgeous empathetic vision. You have been my lifeline so many times. You were God's remedy to the loss of my sister. I love you universes full, my friend!

To Sheila Whittington, thank you from the depths of my heart for coming alongside me, for coaching me, for challenging me, and for helping me find my own true north. Most importantly, thank you for becoming one of my very best friends. Your friendship is full spectrum, and I love you immensely.

To Deanna Wisner, thank you for opening your heart and your home to me. Your loving friendship was like a warm blanket on a cold night. You are a beautifully loving and supportive friend. Thank you for all our couch moments filled with laughter. For every conversation, every tear, and every happy memory made. You are the most understanding and compassionate person I have ever met. Deep gratitude for your friendship.

To Marie Pate, the day I met you a bit of sunshine came back into my life. Thank you for all the joy, all the laughs, and every free haircut you gave me when I had no money. For helping me to feel pretty again, for deep talks, and for all the growing together. I have so much love for you, and your friendship is forever a blessing.

To Shawn Seaton and Brett Stone, thank you for your amazing friendship and for showing up for me in such an unexpected and amazing way. You gave me a lifeline when I needed it most. Our conversations are always so fabulously intelligent. Your kindness will never be forgotten. Your friendship is forever in my heart. Much love for you both.

Rich Parsons, thank you for being my first long-term client. For opening up, for your resolve to pursue the life you want. Such a cool friendship was created from this; you are a truly fab human, and I am blessed to call you friend!

To all of my past relationships, you have been amazing teachers along my path. Thank you for sharing your love and your life with me.

To Ed Maldanado, thank you for your selflessness and generosity in guiding us through the enormously challenging time of Andrew's arrests and court experiences. Without you, I think we would have been lost. Knowing you "had it" was exactly the peace I needed during this vice grip of a year (2011). Thank you, friend!

To every single client I have had the blessing to sit with at the table. You inspire me every single day with your open hearts, courage, and willingness to look at yourself, your business, and your life a different way. It is a privilege to enter this space with you and one that I will never take for granted. Your trust in me is so honoring. Thank you.

To my CHATS Toastmasters family, thank you so very much for setting the bar high and for genuine feedback that was always presented with care and support. Thank you for being this incredible platform that allowed me to overcome throat-clenching fear and find my voice. Thank you for your patience through my speeches that allowed me to heal. You will forever be my family, you will forever be in my heart. Thank you especially to Joel Weldon for your mentorship, Curt Pavlicek for you and your family's beautiful acceptance of us both, and to Kevin Maxwell, Greg Hidder, Tracey Koch, Anne Viseur, Jennifer Carroll, Misty Vogtritter, Kelly Tinberg, Patricia Perna, Neda Kazemi, Jeni Locklin, Daniel Boenning, and so many others whose friendship went beyond meetings.

To Ken Kirk, Taylor Boyd, John Casper, Chad Bays, Byron Johnston, April Hammett, Casey Strunk, and Cody Ritchie, thank you for being a part of my entrance to playing a much bigger game with my coaching and consulting business. And especially to my VA extraordinaire, Rachael Davila, without your help, support, advice, introductions, and trust in bringing me in to work with your people, I wouldn't be where I am today. Much Gratitude.

To Jodi Polanski, Renee Green, Deanne Kimes, Debbie Dumity, and Alexis Bailey, thank you for all the lighthearted moments, happy hours, polo matches, concerts, pool parties, etc. You put such joy into my heart. And Jodi, for stepping on and up with me in our speaking and in our professional pursuits; you still inspire me.

To my Washington Rams of 1980/81, thank you for being the kind of humans that brought me a feeling of belongingness in a time in my life when I needed it before I knew it. Especially Connie Starr, Brady Garrison, Laura Chin, Lisa Teich, Loretta Wilson, Marla Shuster, Kelly Lovin, Jerry Green, and Tom Radic for your lifelong friendships.

To the CCV family, especially Cindy Holly Hesser, Terry Anderson, Dette Derr, Denise Custer, Julie Sabers, Loretta Wilson, Lori Rodriguez, Marti Angst, and Nancy Coughlin, thank you for the beautiful friendship and sharing such a special season of life with me. I have deep love in my heart for all of you, always and forever.

And last but not least… To my Gallup StregthsFinder™, Points of You™, and Collective Gain coaching families, thank you for the knowledge, experience, tools, and inspiration as well as your dedication to better the lives of others. Thank you especially Efrat Shani and Yaron Golan for your commitment to pay it forward, to open hearts and minds in every corner of the world. What you created opened me to the world in a way that I had never before experienced. And to Julija Slaby, you and the amazing way you engaged with us in that room in Half Moon Bay with twenty other beautiful souls from all over the world, this is what sparked the courage in me to speak it out loud, and own the writing of this book.

Made in the USA
Coppell, TX
28 November 2020

42354293R00173